THE SCIENCE
OF RUNNING
A VIRTUAL FAMILY OFFICE

The Journey From Traditional Accountant to Virtual Family Office Professional

ANTON ANDERSON &
PAUL LATHAM

THE
Short Book Formula
PUBLISHING

Published by The Short Book Formula

DISCLAIMER

This book contains the opinions and ideas of the author and is intended for educational and informational purposes only. Careful attention has been paid to ensure the accuracy of the information presented, but the author cannot assume responsibility for the validity or consequences of its use.

The content of this book should not be construed as specific financial, investment, tax, or legal advice. Every individual's financial situation is unique, and readers should consult with qualified professionals who can evaluate their specific circumstances, needs, and goals before making any financial decisions.

The examples, case studies, and scenarios presented in this book are for illustrative purposes only and do not guarantee or predict any particular outcome. Past performance is not indicative of future results. Individual results will vary.

No reader should act or refrain from acting based solely on the information contained in this book without first seeking appropriate professional advice. Any use of the information found in this book is the sole responsibility of the reader. The author, publisher, and any affiliated entities disclaim any liability for actions taken or not taken based on the contents of this book.

Contents

FOREWORD BY

Jared Yellin

Entrepreneurship has always been about one thing for me: creating a life and business that break the mold.

For the past two decades, I've built companies around a simple belief that the future belongs to people willing to think differently, collaborate deeply, and solve bigger problems than everyone else is willing to tackle. Whether through technology, marketing, venture building, or helping entrepreneurs launch and scale businesses, I've learned that the greatest opportunities almost always live where industries are slow to evolve.

The financial services industry is one of those industries.

Most advisors are still operating inside a model that asks them to compete on products, performance, or incremental differentiation. Meanwhile, the clients they serve are facing increasingly complex decisions around taxes, business growth, legacy planning, risk mitigation, and wealth strategy. The gap between what clients need and what most firms are built to deliver continues to widen.

That's what makes The Science of Running a Virtual Family Office so compelling.

Anton Anderson and Paul Latham are not simply presenting another strategy for advisors to grow revenue or gather assets. They are laying out a fundamentally different way to build an advisory business. One centered around collaboration, ecosystem thinking, and creating a level of value that no single professional could deliver alone.

What stood out to me immediately is that this model mirrors what I've seen in every high-performing entrepreneurial venture: the biggest breakthroughs happen when the right people come together around a shared mission. The Virtual Family Office is exactly that. It is a framework for aligning specialists, advisors, and resources around the client in a way that creates deeper trust, stronger outcomes, and more meaningful relationships.

And importantly, this is not theory.

Throughout these pages, Anton and Paul provide practical systems, processes, and real-world examples that show advisors how to actually implement this model. That matters because vision without execution is just noise. The firms that will lead the future of this industry are the ones willing to operationalize collaboration instead of simply talking about it.

I also believe this book speaks to something much bigger than financial services.

At its core, this is about building a business that creates impact at scale. It is about moving beyond transactional relationships and becoming a true architect of opportunity for the families and business owners you serve. That shift changes not only the client experience, but also the trajectory of your business and life.

The future belongs to advisors who stop thinking like isolated practitioners and start building ecosystems that elevate everyone involved.

This book shows you how to do exactly that.

— Jared Yellin

Founder & CEO, Vestige Capital | Entrepreneur & Venture Builder

PART 1

Who This Book Is For

Welcome! This book is aimed at Financial Advisors who currently offer, or seek to offer, financial planning services to wealthy and financially successful clients.

Most Financial Advisors are suffering from the impact of ***"commoditization"*** in their industry.

The typical Advisor "pain" exhibits itself as:

- Struggling to **win *"good"* clients**
- Feeling like they're **selling products** rather than ***"providing a service"***
- Spending a lot of money on **marketing**
- Always **competing** for business - but not *"looking different"*

The **Advisor** feels as though they are stuck in a ***"hamster wheel."***

The typical Advisor worries about where their next client is coming from. They worry about threats that they cannot control; things like artificial intelligence and how it will impact their perceived value. They worry about being "burnt out" by the traditional ways of growing and running a financial advisory practice.

The majority of Advisors (certainly the good ones), understand and recognize that they need to change. However, their key question is **HOW TO CHANGE?**

At Elite (and our associated business – VFO Services), we help Advisors answer that question. We work with them to show them **HOW to *"position themselves"*** with their best clients to be able to demonstrate:

- **Forward-Looking Approach**
  - Helping their clients to achieve their "*big goals*"

- **Proactive Style**
  - Helping their clients make *"smarter decisions"*
  - Helping their clients to protect and grow their wealth

- **Wider Focus – *"Holistic and Comprehensive Advice"***
  - Helping their best clients - who want:
    - Broader scope of services (not just traditional financial planning)
    - Integrated strategic advice, across a wide spectrum
  - They don't want to be *"stuck in narrow advisory silos"*

Financial Advisors need to understand the shifting needs of clients in a rapidly changing market. They need to be aware of the ***"BLAC grid"*** to track changing client perceptions. Where ***"BLAC"*** stands for:

- **B**latant: Is their frustration **obvious?**
- **L**atent: Is their frustration **hidden or emerging?**
- **A**spirational: Is solving their frustration a ***"nice to have"?***
- **C**ritical: Is solving their frustration **urgent?**

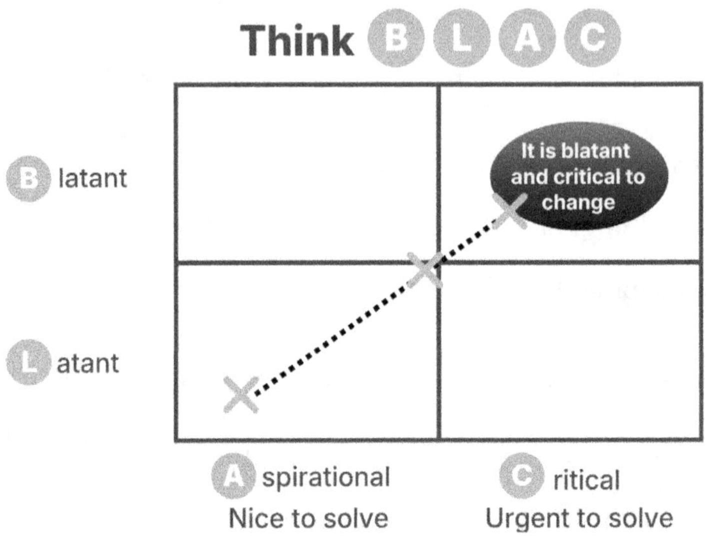

It's not desirable for Financial Advisors to be complacent about their clients in terms of:

- Their frustrations being only **Latent**
- Their desire for change as merely **Aspirational**

Your best clients are no longer positioned in the bottom left quadrant of the above "BLAC" grid.

Today, your wealthy and successful clients are firmly in the top right quadrant. Their frustrations with professional advisors are both **Blatant** and **Critical**. Their need for change and a better professional advice service has become urgent.

This book will open the door to change and a better, more proactive, holistic and comprehensive service.

Whether you choose to use Elite and VFO Services to implement the learnings in the book, or prefer to "do-it-yourself," this book is designed to add value and provide insight on how to run a Virtual Family Office.

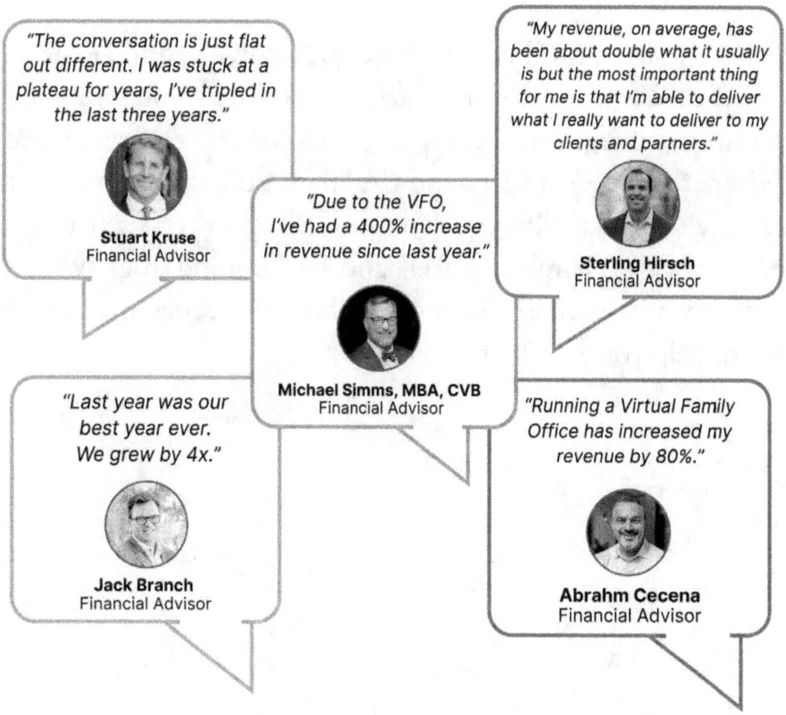

Our Promise to You

We understand that the idea of attracting successful clients by offering a Virtual Family Office service model might seem attractive in theory but, perhaps, unrealistic in practice. We want to reassure you, you are in experienced and capable hands, and the time you invest in reading this book will be well-spent. To demonstrate that experience, we'd like to briefly share our backgrounds and qualifications, helping you understand why (working together) we are uniquely able to provide you with valuable insights and advice.

We have written this book to share our knowledge and experience with you. We promise that, within these pages, you will find the tools and strategies you need to overcome the challenges facing advisors today. We understand the "pain points" and frustrations that advisors face with the "commoditization" of services to the pressure of the "hamster wheel" and the "boiling frog" syndrome. We've both been there "in the trenches," and, together, we know how to help you escape these traps.

Who We Are

Anton Anderson

As a natural-born entrepreneur with a passion for business and finance, I've always been drawn to financial advising. I began my career at Smith Barney but soon realized I wanted a more boutique firm environment. I joined a multi-disciplinary firm in San Diego that offered financial, estate, and tax planning. In 2009, I started my own practice, initially growing it through buying leads, hosting dinner seminars, and radio advertising. After a year, I longed to return to a multi-discipline approach, collaborating with other professionals to grow my practice.

Over the next four years, I embarked on a journey of learning how to work with accountants, attorneys, and other niche specialists participating in nearly a dozen different training programs.

By 2012, things started to click, and my practice grew rapidly by offering clients a multi-disciplinary experience (which, in today's world, would be referred to as a "Virtual Family Office").

In 2014, I exited my individual practice and co-founded Elite Resource Team. The mission was to take what we had learned and help financial advisors differentiate themselves in a crowded and competitive market. As a Consultant, Investor, and Thought Leader, I have trained over 1,200 advisors across forty states, teaching them how to form accountant partnerships and leverage the power of a Virtual Family Office. I have also co-authored two Amazon bestselling books on related topics, "The Art of Collaboration" and "The Art of Proactivity."

Paul Latham

In our previous books, *"The Art of Collaboration"* and the *"Art of Proactivity,"* I explained the story of Lathams Accountants in the UK.

It was at Lathams where I first began to understand the power of teamwork. Our best clients were able to access expert resources, capable of implementing a wide range of solutions to meet their diverse needs.

In the late 20th Century, nobody used the term "Virtual Family Office." It was a pre-internet age, after all. However, essentially, that was the service we were providing at Lathams. In fact, I show a copy below of an original business vision document (dated 1999), that describes how Lathams offered what we called a "Gateway to everything that growing/changing owner managed businesses might need."

Having sold Lathams in 2001 and pursued various other business interests after that, I moved to the USA in 2011 mainly to "have a lifestyle change."

Having moved, I quickly realized that US Accountants needed help to escape their commoditization and differentiate themselves. I formed HaydenRock Solutions, initially to help those Accountants offer Business Advisory Services to their best clients. This eventually led to meeting Anton and merging HaydenRock Solutions with Elite Resource Team.

As Anton describes above, in the immediate pre/post covid period, we continued to work hard to help Advisors and Accountants to leverage the Power of a Virtual Family Office. In that period, Elite

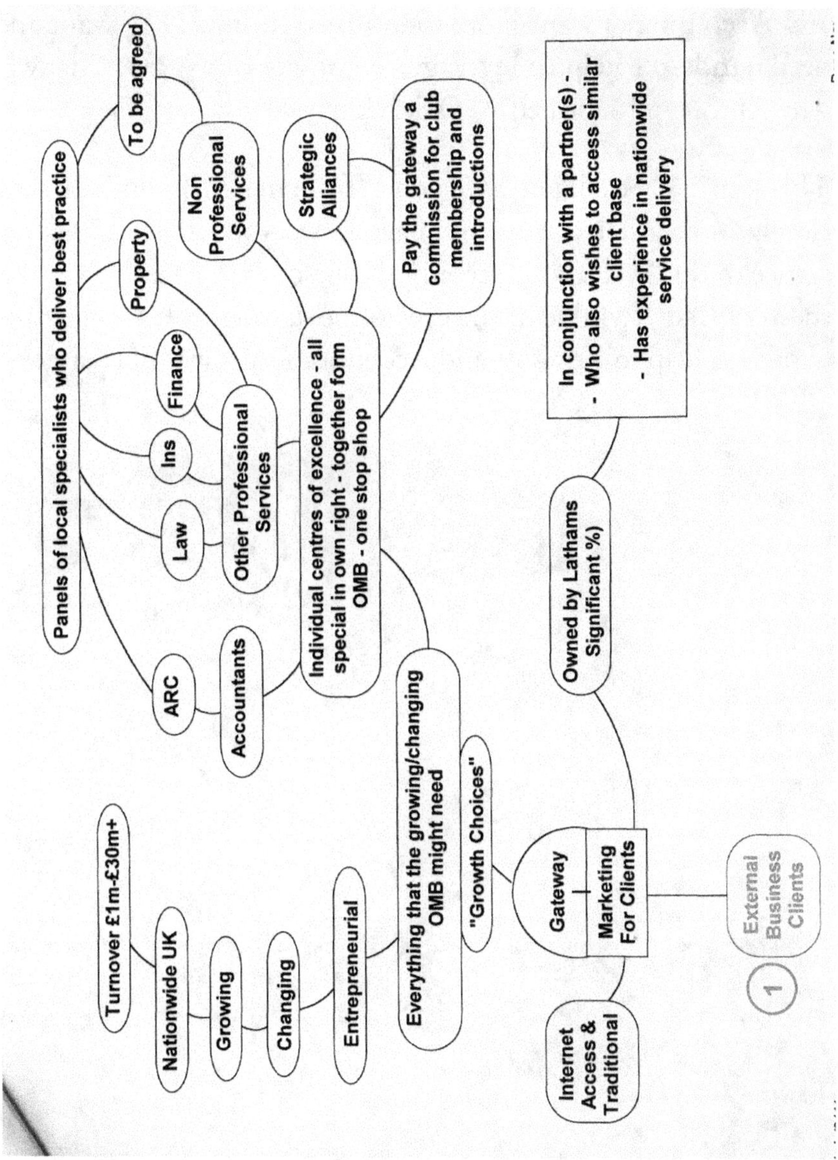
Turnover £1m-£30m+
Nationwide UK
Growing
Changing
Entrepreneurial
Everything that the growing/changing OMB might need
"Growth Choices"
Internet Access & Traditional
Gateway
Marketing For Clients
External Business Clients
1
Panels of local specialists who deliver best practice
ARC
Accountants
Law
Ins
Finance
Property
Other Professional Services
Non Professional Services
To be agreed
Strategic Alliances
Individual centres of excellence - all special in own right - together form OMB - one stop shop
Pay the gateway a commission for club membership and introductions
Owned by Lathams Significant %)
In conjunction with a partner(s) -
- Who also wishes to access similar client base
- Has experience in nationwide service delivery

Resource Team was very much a **training company.**

We describe below our recognition that many (in fact, most) Advisors and Accountants want more than just training. They want and need **hands-on-help to leverage the power of a VFO.** That was why Anton and I formed VFO Services.

This journey feels like I have gone "full circle." If you look very closely at the vision document image above, you will see a brief reference to the "ARC" or "Accountant Resource Center." That was the very first "twinkle in the eye" of how, today, we provide that hands-on-help to Advisors and Accountants using VFO Services.

Elite Resource Team and Virtual Family Office Services

Before we get into the details of the book, we need to explain the relationship between Elite and VFO Services (and the reason why Anton and Paul founded VFO Services).

Whilst it is VFO Services that is at "front and center" in much of this book, it was Elite Resource Team that was the original **Member Training Business** for the Team Based Model. We previously explained in the ***"Art of Collaboration"*** how the **Team Based Model** worked, and how that was hugely beneficial for Advisors (and Accountants) who were **willing to put in the *"hard yards"*** to **integrate the model** into their business.

However, Anton and Paul recognized the need for a **faster and easier solution** that was particularly aimed at the needs of already successful, busy Advisors who had the platform to grow further and wanted a more "turnkey" solution.

Those Advisors could immediately see the **vision.** They could see how the VFO could potentially help them generate new planning revenues and simultaneously differentiate themselves when winning more traditional Advisor business.

However, only being able to see the vision is simply not sufficient. As Paul likes to say, there are ***"3 ingredients of business success,"*** and it is the combination of **Vision x Plan x Desire = Business Success.**

The problem was that many busy Advisors simply do not have the time to spend months and years ***"mastering the rules like a pro"*** that are required to be able to run a VFO and ***"do-it-themselves."***

Advisors usually need assistance, and in particular, most benefit from a ***"short-cut"*** on the **Plan** and **Desire** elements of the business success "equation."

That was Anton and Paul's initial "ah-hah moment" and when the idea of VFO Services was first conceived.

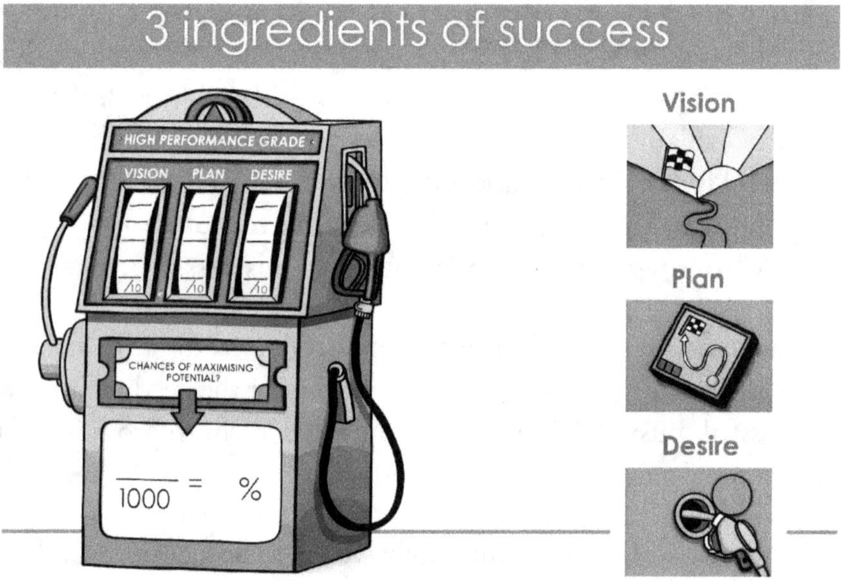

Anton and Paul also understood a **second, critical part of the required game-plan**. The Team Based Model works best when the Advisor is able to create a business structure that at Elite we call ***"2 Businesses Under 1 Roof."***

This concept applies in many businesses, certainly Accountant businesses, and was discussed at length in the ***"Art of Proactivity."*** It also (almost always) applies to Financial Advisors, too.

Essentially, the Advisor need for ***"2 Businesses Under 1 Roof"*** follows their understanding that, when Advisors want to integrate the VFO, there is a clear and fundamental need to **SEPARATE** (their traditional core business from the added-value VFO).

- Having separated - they are then able to **CONNECT** their best clients (to that VFO business) when appropriate.

Let us explain further.

Advisors who join Elite have previously established their traditional core business (specific services will vary by Advisor). By way of simple explanation, their core business might be (say) ***"AUM and Financial Planning Business"*** or ***"AUM"*** for short.

The first goal of any Advisor is to **grow their core business**. We all know this is a ***"commodity"*** **business** (and, obviously, please don't misunderstand the point we are making. We 100% know it also provides value) – but to directly quote one successful Elite Advisor their first goal might be best expressed as:

- **Goal 1**- *"Keep the core business boring and scalable"*

However, that same advisor added a second goal, **recognizing the need to differentiate and add further value via the Virtual Family Office.**

- **Goal 2** – *"Provide proactive planning to complex clients"*
    - Delivered by the Team Based Model via VFO

It should be obvious that to totally integrate both goals into a single business would create confusion. We would see problems like:

- Charging fees for Goal 1 that also somehow cover Goal 2
  - Where different team members not involved in the core
    - This problem is further exacerbated once you recognize that not every client wanting core services will also want wider VFO services.
- Recognizing the Advisor doesn't want unnecessary *"friction or ambiguity"*
  - To quote that same Advisor again

In fact, "ambiguity" happens because of the **lack of clear separation between Goal 1 and Goal 2** (but with appropriate client connection to the "boutique" as shown by the arrow in the illustration below).

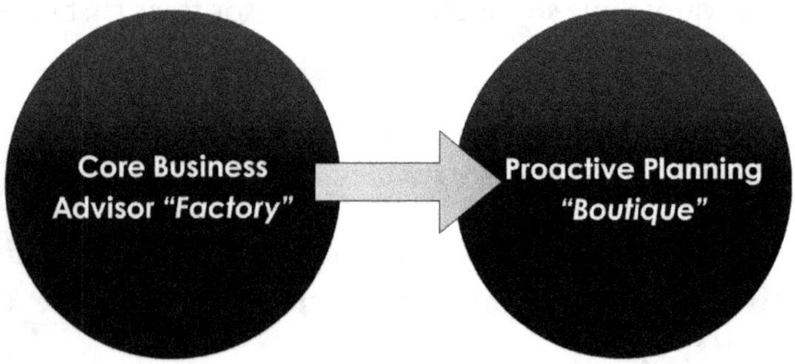

When an Advisor does not separate into two clear operating areas, their value proposition may become confusing and "jumbled" to the client.

- As an example, in the VFO value proposition it is highly appropriate to describe your VFO team's *"holistic"* approach. However, that *"holistic"* word is not required and not appropriate when talking purely about the core business (operating in a narrow *"silo"* – and not *"holistic"* by definition).

Key Difference between Goal 1 and Goal 2 at a High Level

- **Core Advisor Business** – focused mostly on **EFFICIENT** delivery
    - Think of this like a *"factory"*
        - Grow by increasing volume of (example) AUM efficiently
- **VFO Business** – focused entirely on **VALUE ADDED** delivery
    - Think of this like a *"planning boutique"*
        - Grow by adding value and solving complex problems

It is actually very hard for an individual Advisor to "straddle" both of the above simultaneously (without VFO Services to provide "hands-on" help). As Paul Latham says, for an individual Advisor to try to do both, generally results in ***"Monday to Friday syndrome."***

- On Monday, I will be efficient – and on Tuesday, I will add value – and on Wednesday, I will be efficient – and on Thursday, I will add value – and by Friday . . . we are likely not maximizing performance.

To maximize the probability of success and to make this second VFO (proactive planning) business easy for Advisors to implement, is the secondary reason why VFO Services was created by Anton and Paul.

- VFO Services allows Advisors to ***"bolt-on their Planning Boutique"***
- VFO Services does all the ***"heavy lifting."*** It provides:
    - Value Proposition – to win new work
    - *"Front of House"* Planning Team – facilitate the client discussion
    - *"Behind the Scenes"* - Planning Team - liaison with VFO Specialists
    - Efficient administration, billing, and client communication
- Advisor is positioned as ***"orchestrator"*** – main role to ***"hand-hold"* client**

The introduction of VFO Services now provides the Advisor not only with the **Vision** but also the **Plan** already in place – and the **Desire** to implement is reduced from months and years to literally days and weeks.

The chances of Maximizing Potential are dramatically increased.

- In fact, in the first six months of introducing VFO Services, Anton and Paul discovered that the Advisor success rate was increased by 392% (in terms of VFO dollars generated), compared to the traditional *"DIY"* approach to integrating the Team Based Model and was also 154% more effective than when the Advisors chose to work with an Elite Coach to help *"stiffen and sustain their desire."*

It was clear to Anton and Paul that their "ah-hah moment" was going to provide a winning formula for those busy Advisors who "got the vision" immediately but simply didn't have the time to create the plan and implement it with sustained desire. **VFO Services** was a ***"game changer."***

Through this book, you will see references to both Elite Resource Team and VFO Services. Very simplistically:

- **Elite Resource Team** provides the **initial training** for the Advisor
    - Together with the community for more **effective collaboration**

- **VFO Services** provides *"hands on"* **delivery of service to Advisor's clients**

One final point, this book is intended to help you whether you want to:

- Implement the learnings yourself and ***"do-it-yourself"*** or:
- Work with VFO Services to provide ***"hands on"*** **help**

In this book we have tried to show you enough detail, so that you ***"get it"*** **and properly understand the context of how you will be working with clients.**

If you are planning on the ***"DIY"*** **route,** it would be tedious to go through every single "nut and bolt and nuance" required to run a successful VFO. This book will give you enough context to understand what you will need to do. We will then supplement this book with a detailed **Elite Training Manual** (that does go through every single "nut, bolt and nuance" required). You will also likely benefit from the **Frequently Asked Questions** at the back of the book.

Equally, if you are planning on the **VFO Services *"Fast Track"* route,** it would be a very short and, to be honest, no more than a marketing book if we only covered the parts that require the Advisor to do or say something personally. We are obviously going to cover those specifics in this book, but we are also going to provide some brief context of what the VFO Team will also be doing at each stage to help you achieve a successful outcome with clients.

That is why this book is called the ***"Science of Running a Virtual Family Office."***

Having explained the above, it is time to move to Part 2 and focus on the specific type of Advisor you are.

PART 2

What Type of Financial Advisor Are You?

You Require a "*Compliance Driven*" Vision. Very simplistically there are three broad types of Financial Advisor:

- Those who have a vision to offer wider advice to their best clients (via the Virtual Family Office) – and are:

1. **Not overly constrained** by compliance factors
2. **Somewhat constrained** by compliance factors
   - Can offer wider advice via VFO but cannot accept revenue share from VFO Specialists
3. **Very constrained** by compliance factors:
   - Cannot offer wider advice via VFO regardless of revenue share arrangements

At Elite and VFO Services, we offer different "Fast Track" type solutions for each of the above types of Financial Advisor.

If you are the type of Financial Advisor who is **not overly constrained by compliance factors** (either **Type 1** or possibly **Type 2** above), then this is definitely the book for you.

- ***"The Art of Running a Virtual Family Office"***

If you are the type of Financial Advisor who is **very constrained by compliance factors** (definitely Type 3 above), then this book may not be the best starting point for you. You will likely be more interested in our "sister publication."

- ***"The Art of Building Accountant Partnerships"***

Two Things to Know About Fast Track

Whichever of the two books that you are reading, there are two things to know about the ***"VFO Fast Track"*** services, they are both:

- **Fast**
  - Designed to **achieve fast results**
- **On a Track**
  - Process driven, and designed to make them **easy to implement**

PART 3

Running a VFO "*Fast Track*" Executive Summary

In summary, what is a Virtual Family Office, and what does running it with the benefit of a "*Fast Track*" approach mean in this context?

Virtual Family Office

An Advisor providing their clients access to a VFO massively differentiates themselves from the traditional competition. A VFO brings together professionals across multiple disciplines, as shown next.

Those different **VFO Specialists** are **collaborating** with **Members and Clients** in a **virtual environment** to deliver comprehensive, coordinated, proactive advice. We discuss this in more detail later, but it's the same concept as the family offices used by billionaire families like the Rockefellers (starting in the 19th century) through to the Waltons (just as applicable today in the 21st century). The key difference with a VFO is the word ***"virtual,"*** **that makes the traditional family office accessible to your best clients** (see below for ideal client types).

Elite Resource Team is North America's largest Virtual Family Office provider, serving over 1,200 Financial Advisors and Accountants nationwide. The VFO enables Advisors and

Accountants to offer billionaire-level family office services to their clients through our extensive team of more than seventy-five vetted specialists. However, rather than requiring "billionaire" clients, the VFO serves the more typical "mass-affluent," "high-net-worth," and successful business owner clients.

VFO, combined with a *"Fast Track"* Approach to Client Service by combining the benefit of the VFO with the efficiency of a process and a client experience-driven service, VFO Fast Track helps Advisors generate new VFO Revenues very quickly (on average thirty-nine days after starting training) and successfully. As discussed, at the outset, Advisors can use the learnings to "do-it-themselves." However, the benefits of the "fast track style" approach are clear. Either way, ERT provide the initial training, but:

- **VFO Services work with you and your clients - they:**
    - Attend the client meetings
    - Lead and facilitate the proactive conversations
    - Present the Virtual Family Office
    - Handle client objections
    - Help you close the business
    - Deal with all client billing and administration of monies collected

Breaking those thirty-nine days down further. On average it takes:

- Twenty-two days to complete the initial training for VFO Fast Track

- Seventeen days to generate the first **Tax Planning Fees**
    - Generating the first ***Holistic Planning*** **Fees** can extend those thirty-nine days to fifty days from starting training

CONSISTENT MEASURABLE RESULTS

89%
Of advisors in the program generate VFO revenue after introducing at least one client

$4,786
Average holistic revenue per client

$22,205
Average tax planning revenue per client

There is a key point there. You need to introduce clients to the program . . . and don't stop after training! Advisors must still bring "some" **DESIRE** to achieve **Vision and Growth Plan**.

The Average Revenue per client (above) consists of a mix of:

- Average Tax Planning Fees **$22,205**
- Average *Holistic Planning* Fees (blended average of Lite and Core) **$4,786**
    - Excludes additional VFO Revenues generated via VFO Specialists

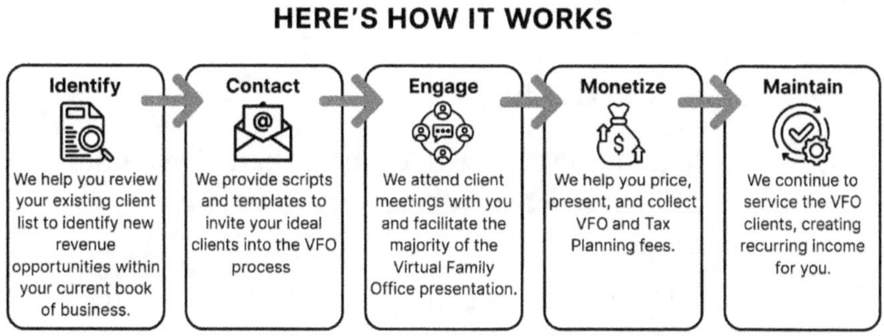

The *"secret sauce"* of VFO Fast Track is how we Engage Target Clients

We will show you in Part 5 how to identify target clients, and in Part 6, how to contact them (and invite them to experience the proactive process), but the biggest difference maker with VFO FT is the **Engage** step. That's the ***"done-for-you"*** and ***"hands-on"*** part with your client.

The main reason that the results (shown above) are so quick and consistent, is because the VFO Services Team are **already trained and practiced.** They are "slick and professional" – which means that all Advisors do is "hold your client's hand" through the process.

From the client perspective, the Advisor appears to be "leading and orchestrating," but in fact, the **VFO Services team are doing all the *"heavy lifting"* for you.**

VFO Fast Track Program includes:

- **Condensed Training**
  - Elite traditionally provided more than ninety hours of content to learn and use - in a *"DIY"* style – with your clients.
    - VFO FT has condensed that to only **3.5 hours of training**

- **Proprietary Client Scripts**
  - Means you **know exactly what to say** – both to:
    - Set up client meetings
    - Introduce VFO Services as your planning team

- **Facilitating the Proactive Discussions**
  - You introduce VFO Services – they lead the presentation
    - Practiced and professional
    - Doing all the ***"heavy lifting"***

- **Accessing the Virtual Family Office**
  - VFO Services **provide the gateway** to more than seventy-five professional VFO Specialists – across all five areas
    - Vetted and highly skilled
    - Revenue sharing agreements in place

Ideal Clients for VFO Fast Track

The VFO FT program works best with three types of clients:

- ***"Mass-Affluent"***
  - Annual Income – typically more than $250,000
  - Assets – typically more than $500,000 (excluding home)
- ***"High-Net-Worth"***
  - Annual Income – will vary by region across different parts of USA
  - Assets – starting point $1 million (excluding home)
- ***"Successful Business Owners"***
  - Annual Revenue – minimum $1 million (ideally more)
  - *"Proper Business"* – with *"desire to grow"* not *"lifestyle"* / *"hobby"*

Tips for Success in VFO Fast Track Program

Our most successful Advisors demonstrate some common traits which are detailed below:

- Commit to Process
  - Typically, two hours per week
    - Initially in training
    - Then introducing clients to process
  - Designed for busy Advisors
    - ***"Consistency beats intensity"***

- Follow the Process
  - Called "*Fast Track*" for a reason!
    - We enjoy a high close rate
      - *"Trust the process – it works"*
- Use the Scripts
  - Our scripts are tried – tested – and proven!
    - *"Don't be tempted to reinvent the wheel"*
- Identify "*Best Fit*" Clients First
  - Start with five clients where you already have a good relationship
    - Fitting the ideal client descriptions above
      - *"Your clients will thank you for trying to add value"*
- **Allow VFO Services to Lead Meetings**
  - Show up prepared – and introduce us
    - VFO Services handle the majority of presentation
      - ***"Your only job is to just hand-hold the client"***
- **Leverage the VFO Services Team**
  - The team are committed to making this a success for you
    - ***"Behind the scenes is where the true complexity is navigated and the magic happens"***
- **Fully Leverage the VFO**
  - Don't limit yourself to only one or two "*favorite*" specialists

    - All five areas of VFO create opportunities and client value
        - ***"Think singles and doubles – not just home runs"***

- **Stay Active in the Elite Community**
    - All our Advisors have been where you are at one time (just starting)
        - Collaborate with successful advisors – and learn from them
            - ***"Success is literally at your fingertips"***

Compensation Structure of VFO Fast Track

Advisors always retain **100% of revenue from all regulated activities**, to include:

- Assets Under Management (AUM) fees
- Financial Planning fees
- Life Insurance commissions
- Annuity commissions
- All other securities, and traditional insurance product compensation

There is no revenue sharing arrangement on securities transactions, traditional insurance products, or financial planning services.

VFO Specialist revenues, for services outside the Advisor's core offering, are **shared with the Advisor where compliance allows**.

A key factor is that **VFO Services** are **only remunerated upon your success** (as well as working towards the success of your client and with VFO Specialists). VFO Services are incentivized to ***"make this process work"*** for you – your clients – the VFO Specialists – as well as ourselves. Our goal is truly to create a ***"win-win-win-win"*** **scenario for all stakeholders.**

Comparing Traditional Style Advisory with using VFO

If we make a comparison between the traditional Advisor situation and using VFO Fast Track:

- **Without the VFO** versus working with the **VFO**
    - Limited to services you traditionally offer
        - *Now offer comprehensive family office services*
    - Miss revenue opportunities outside your personal expertise
        - ***Capture new revenue streams via VFO Specialist***
    - Clients seek help elsewhere for complex needs
        - ***Become client's most relevant contact or "go-to"***

PART 4

Further Understanding the Virtual Family Office

Origins of a Family Office

Once upon a time, there was the Rockefeller Family. Let us start to get into detail with regard to the VFO by taking you back in time to 1882.

That was when the Rockefeller Family first created the concept of a "Family Office."

The Rockefeller Family was frustrated because they had numerous and various professional specialists, but they were **providing conflicting advice** to the family.

The Rockefellers **decided to make a change**. They interviewed dozens of professionals to find the best of the best and then offered to hire them to work exclusively as their full-time employees. The goal was to create a team that could provide the family with the **best holistic advice and the best possible outcomes and solutions.**

This "Family Office" concept quickly caught on with other wealthy families.

Modern day family offices are used by ultra high net worth families, including people like Oprah and Reed Hastings from Netflix and families like the Bloombergs and Waltons. Although the family offices are incredibly valuable, they are also incredibly expensive to run, with an annual cost ranging from a few million to hundreds of millions a year! Why would they pay that much? Because the value of having all of their professionals collaborate on their behalf far exceeds the cost.

Obviously, these family offices are a great benefit to ultra wealthy families. Unfortunately, they are not an option for most people because of the cost of employing the professionals. But the internet and the virtual world has removed that obstacle, completely.

Modern Day Family Offices[2]

Kylie Jenner
Cosmetics/Celebrity
Net Worth: $700M+
Est. Cost: $1-3M

Michael Jordan
Basketball Legend
Net Worth: $3.2B
Est. Cost: $5M-$15M

Jeff Bezos
Amazon
Net Worth: $250B
Est. Cost: $350M

Walton Family
Walmart
Net Worth: $250B
Est. Cost: $350M-$500M

Birth of the Virtual Family Office

The internet has been a *"game-changer."*

Today at Elite (and for clients working with VFO Services trained professional members), the "Virtual Family Office" uses the same foundational concept as a traditional Family Office, which is to have **specialists across five broad professional disciplines**, which are:

- Advanced Tax Planning
- Wealth Management
- Legal Services
- Business Advisory
- Risk Mitigation

The VFO specialists all collaborate with our trained professional Members in a virtual environment to **deliver that proactive, holistic and comprehensive advice to successful clients**.

Effectively, the VFO provides a **wider resource to serve client needs**.

Those five areas (detailed above) are obviously extremely diverse, and it would be impossible for most individual professional firms to be able to offer true expertise and specialist help across all of them.

Elite has spent a decade building their VFO and is comprised of more than seventy-five individual ***"VFO Specialists."***

To help make this more tangible, below are examples for each of the five areas: [1]

Tax Planning

- Examples Strategies
    - Cash Balance Plan
    - Accountable Plan
    - Augusta Rule
    - Entity Election
    - Tax Loss Harvesting
    - Solar Funds
    - Section 179 Expensing
    - Deferred Compensation
    - 1031 Exchange
    - Opportunity Zones
    - Charitable Remainder Trusts

Risk Mitigation

- P&C Insurance
- Captive Insurance
- Living too Long
- Dying too Soon
- Physical Accidents
- Theft

Wealth Management

- Financial Planning
- Investment Management
    - Retirement planning
    - Alternative investments
    - Real estate
    - Cryptocurrencies
    - Art
    - NFTs

Legal Services

- Estate Planning
- Entity Formation
- Contract Creation
- Resolving Disputes
- Regulatory Compliance
- Mergers & Acquisitions
- Employment Law

Business Advisory

- Strategic Planning
- Financial Management
- Operational Improvement
- Performance Measurement
- Succession Planning
- Technology Transformation
- Growth and Expansion Strategies

Elite and VFO Services also have a full time employee (called "VFO Liaison") whose only job is to manage the relationships with these specialists and help professionals in the Elite Community to become comfortable and work with them effectively with their clients.

To allow easy access to the VFO, we create a **Team-Based Model** structure that looks like the illustration on the next page, where, as you can see, that model is comprised of **two collaborative teams:**

- **Proactive Planning Team**
- **Virtual Family Office Specialists**

Both teams are important in terms of **providing the holistic and comprehensive service** needed to best service clients.

We go into more detail in Part 7, when we talk about how we **Engage** clients in "Holistic Planning."

PART 5

Identify Target Clients

At VFO Services we use a five-step process in VFO Fast Track, which is shown below.

We previously covered in Part 3 the key attributes of the ideal target clients. The reason that we consider them "right" is because these are the three types that offer the most opportunity working with the Virtual Family Office. To remind you those types may be summarized as:

- ***"Mass-Affluent"***
    - Annual Income – typically over $250,000
        - Assets – typically over $500,000 (excluding home)
- *"High-Net-Worth"*
    - Annual Income – will vary by region across different parts of USA
        - Assets – starting point $1 million (excluding home)
- ***"Successful" Business Owners***
    - Annual Revenue – minimum $1 million (ideally more)
        - *"Proper Business"* – with "*desire to grow*" not "*lifestyle*" / "*hobby*"

You now simply need to go through your clients to identify the "right types" and put them on your client tracker list.

If you are planning on ***"doing this yourself,"*** Elite can provide you with a simple client tracker template.

If you are working with **VFO Services**, we will upload your clients onto the **VFO Fast Track** client tracker, which then tracks your clients through every single step that is covered in the remainder of this book (and a lot more detail that is not covered in this book, but which can be found in the VFO Services Fast Track Training Manual).

If as a result of this exercise, you discover that you don't have enough clients of the "right type," and you want to get access to more target clients, then you should perhaps read our sister publication, ***"The Art of Building Accountant Partnerships."*** This is the perfect way to generate more client targets. We call it ***"fishing with a big net."***

Having identified the target clients, you need to invite them to engage in the process. This is covered in Part 6.

PART 6

Contact Target Clients

This is the second step below in the five-step process for VFO Fast Track. This can be broken into some simple steps as follows:

Email Template to Client

The ideal time to send the email is at the beginning of the week (likely a Monday), and it is very short, just *"planting the seed"* in the mind of the client. We are letting them know that we will be following up to call them later.

The email subject line should be ***"Widening my focus,"*** and the content is as follows:

> Dear XXX,
>
> In addition to providing my traditional financial planning, I have aligned with a **Virtual Family Office that specializes in advanced tax planning and business advisory services.**
>
> This will provide my clients with more choice and deeper resources.
>
> I'm excited to tell you more, and I will be reaching out soon to arrange a mutually convenient time to meet.
>
> Regards,

You will see from the above that the Advisor is not pretending that they are suddenly doing this alone. They make it clear that this is essentially a ***"joint venture"*** with a separate Virtual Family Office provider.

As a comment, if a particular target client is not a business owner, then you can still leave it as shown above. Alternatively, you might tailor it to add something else from the VFO that may be of more interest to a particular target (example, estate planning or legal services).

Having sent that email out on (say) Monday or Tuesday, you will follow it up with a phone call (see below).

Telephone Script to Client

This telephone call to the client to follow up, should be made (ideally) no more than two days after the original email above. The script looks like this:

> Hey (client's name) how are you? Great to hear.
>
> As you read in my email, we are enhancing our services for our best clients and transitioning to a more proactive approach. We have heard over the last few years that our clients really prefer this forward looking service.
>
> Seeing that you are one of our best clients, I would like to schedule a Zoom meeting so I can introduce you to our Proactive Planning Team and walk you through our Proactive Planning Process.
>
> To make sure we have enough time to walk through things, I'd like to set aside sixty minutes. It may end up being shorter, but let's just be safe and plan on sixty minutes.
>
> I'm available ______ or _______ . What works best for you? Perfect! Let's book that.
>
> In addition to that initial meeting, I'd like to also set a short follow up meeting two days later. It'll be less than thirty minutes and will just give us a chance to discuss any questions that may have come up since the initial meeting.
>
> So for that thirty minutes, I'm available ____ or ____ . What works best for you? Perfect! Let's book that as well.
>
> I'll make sure we get you an invite out with the Zoom details. Please just accept that invite, so we know you got it.
>
> I look forward to seeing you on _____ day, at _____ time.

Note: Make sure an email confirmation is sent with meeting time/date/location

Some important points are highlighted below:

Some Advisors say they prefer to skip the email template and move directly into a telephone call. That is your prerogative, but statistical evidence proves that it is typically better to send the email first to "plant the seed" with the client in advance.

The script covers arranging two meetings:

- **Initial Partners in Planning (PIP) Introduction Meeting**
  - This is covered in Part 7 - Engaging Holistic Planning Clients
- **PIP Follow Up Meeting**
  - This is covered in Part 9 - Monetizing the Engagement
  - It particularly allows time to agree the fee to be quoted

In practice the Initial Meeting may be less than sixty minutes, but this time means that we will definitely finish.

Similarly, the Follow Up meeting may be less than thirty minutes, but this means we will definitely finish, and in particular, have time to discuss the Service Membership Fee options properly.

It is hugely important that you arrange both meetings during this call - as the **two meetings need to be ideally no more than two to three days apart.**

If the meetings are not arranged together, and they are arranged longer apart, the **percent closing rate will be significantly worse** (as the client will simply not remember in the Follow Up Meeting what was discussed in the Initial Meeting).

Obviously, in the event that the client prefers not to continue to the Follow Up Meeting, it is **easy to cancel the second meeting**. However, by contrast, it is **generally impossible to arrange the second meeting at short notice after the Initial Meeting** (in fact VFO Services will not proceed unless both meetings are arranged in advance, as we know from experience that we would be "wasting everybody's time" to do so).

We are now ready to move to **Part 7 - Engage in *Holistic Planning***.

PART 7

Engage with Target Clients - ***Holistic Planning***

Team Based Model and Proactive Process

As we briefly introduced previously in Part 4, at VFO Services, when we first engage with a client, the goal is to help the client to:

- Understand and Prioritize Client **Needs**
- Address their Biggest **Problems**
- Achieve their Most Important **Priority Goals**

And to remind you, the Team Based Model is comprised of **two collaborative teams:**

- **Proactive Planning Team** (team provided by VFO Services)
- **Virtual Family Office Specialists**

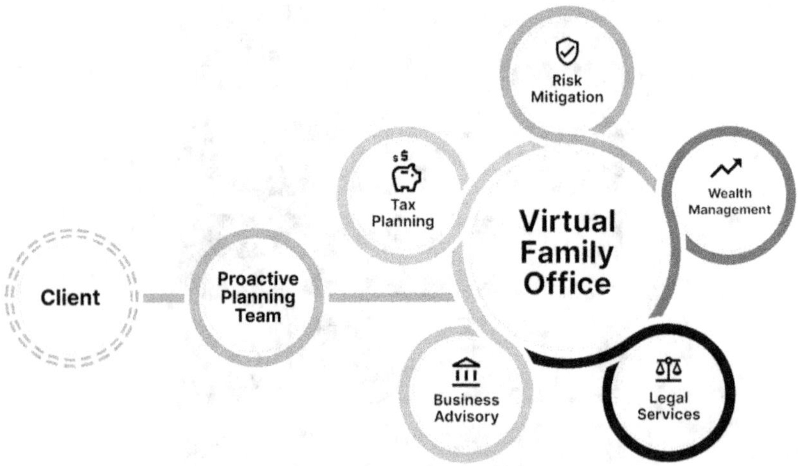

Let us now look at how the teams work in more detail.

Proactive Planning Team

The Proactive Planning Team is divided into **two parts of the same team.** They are best visualized as *"front office"* and *"back office"* (in terms of their different relationships with the client).

The **Proactive Planning Team *"Front Office"* works directly with the client**, typically via zoom meetings together.

We position the "front office" of the Proactive Planning Team as the client's ***"eyes and ears"*** when it comes to offering a proactive planning service.

When we first engage with the client, the client will typically meet **two team members** in the "front of house."

Proactive Planning Team

CLIENT RELATIONSHIP / ADVANCED PLANNING LEAD
[Name]
Your planning team leader

PROACTIVE FACILITATOR
[Name]
Initial diagnostic & prioritization of opportunities

- **Client Relationship Lead**
    - Usually this is the **Financial Advisor**.
        - You lead the relationship with your client exactly as normal.
            - *Aside from "holding your client's hand," you will not be expected to do any "heavy lifting." You can leave that to the rest of the Proactive Planning Team* (via VFO Services).
                - **Advisors require very little training**, aside from understanding the process in overview.

- **Proactive Facilitator**
    - The Proactive Facilitator role is to lead the client through the process of identifying and prioritizing their planning needs (more of that later in the book when we discuss the process in more detail).
        - The key point to understand is that VFO Services facilitators are extensively trained and heavily practiced in presenting the process to clients.
            - This is a fundamental reason why results are achieved so quickly in VFO Fast Track, as "practice makes perfect."

Where the Client requires **Tax Planning** (more than 80% of the time), we typically add a third "front of house" team member to the Proactive Planning Team.

- **Director of Advanced Tax Planning**
    - The Director of Advanced Planning (a CPA with more than twenty-five years of professional experience) works on creating a high-level tax plan with the client, aimed at maximizing their tax savings and return on investment.

- We adopt a step-by-step approach to tax planning, backed by strong guarantees, that allow the client to move at their own pace and always feel *"comfortable and in control."*
- Once the high-level plan has been agreed with the client, the Director of Advanced Planning introduces the appropriate VFO Tax Specialists to help implement the specific tax strategies (as detailed in the high-level plan).

The Advisor's main role in this Initial Planning Meeting will be to make the introductions. Here is the script of what you will say on the first two slides.

> As I mentioned in my invitation - I am looking forward to sharing some exciting updates with you. Big picture - what we're going to walk through is in addition to everything I've historically done for my clients, so it's above and beyond that - and is completely optional.
>
> I'm sharing it with you because I've had a number of clients over the last few years request more proactive and advanced planning across both their personal and business landscapes, and I've finally found the team to be able to offer it.
>
> Now, before we get started, I should mention that with me today as part of my team is [PROACTIVE FACILITATOR NAME]. He is an important part of delivering a wider and more proactive range of services to clients.
>
> [PROACTIVE FACILITATOR NAME] before you introduce yourself, as a way of introduction this is [CLIENT NAME]. I've known [CLIENT NAME] for (amount of time) and they... (advisor adds something unique about the client.

For example, "We originally met through our kids' soccer team, and I've really enjoyed working with them because they are always open to learning and follow through on our conversations.") Allow room for the client to reply.

With that said, [PROACTIVE FACILITATOR NAME] can you introduce yourself to [CLIENT NAME]?

[PROACTIVE FACILITATOR]: "Thanks [ADVISOR NAME], [CLIENT NAME] it's nice to meet you. I am excited to be part of [ADVISOR NAME]'s team."

Perfect [PROACTIVE FACILITATOR NAME], thanks for that. So let's get started.

ADVISOR CONTINUES

[CLIENT NAME] I have decided to introduce my clients to a new service - it is called the Virtual Family Office - and they help me offer a significantly wider planning focus compared to the typical financial advisor. [PROACTIVE FACILITATOR NAME] do you want to walk [CLIENT NAME] through it?

Aside from the above, the Advisor has nothing further to say in the presentation, apart from a couple of pre-scripted places where they add a short comment (when prompted to do so by the Proactive Facilitator).

As well as the "front office," behind the scenes in the "back office" of the Proactive Planning Team, you will discover that there are two more key roles, the **VFO Liaison** and the **Proactive Coordinator**.

You will almost never see these people in person, but they both play a vital role (we will detail later). For now, it is important to understand that it's a combination of the "front office" and "back office" teamwork that results in the true magic of the VFO model.

When we first engage with the client, we run through an outline presentation that starts with explaining the origins of the Family Office and how a VFO works today. We previously covered this in Part 4.

Proactive Planning Team Connects Seamlessly to VFO

We explain that the VFO is basically a big technical resource, providing solutions for professionals and their clients, where, as you walk through the entrance:

- On the right are all the **business planning focus areas**
- On the left are all the **personal planning focus areas**

Virtual Family Office Showroom

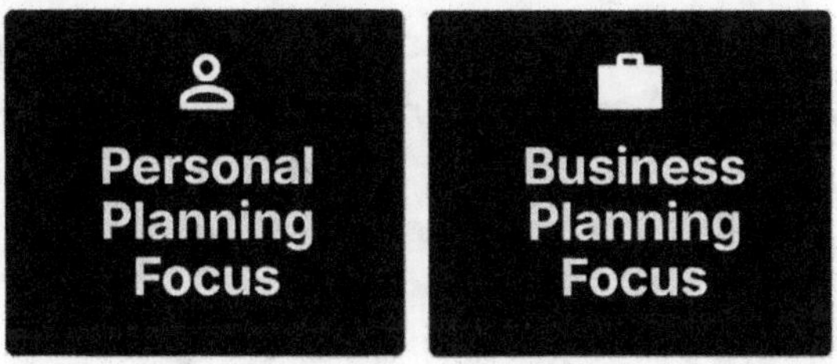

Starting with the **Personal Planning side of the VFO Showroom**, we suggest to the client that they should think of the larger titles at the top of each box (shown below) as being like the "aisles in the showroom."

The image below shows only some of those solutions – it's just a snapshot.

Virtual Family Office Showroom

Personal Planning Focus

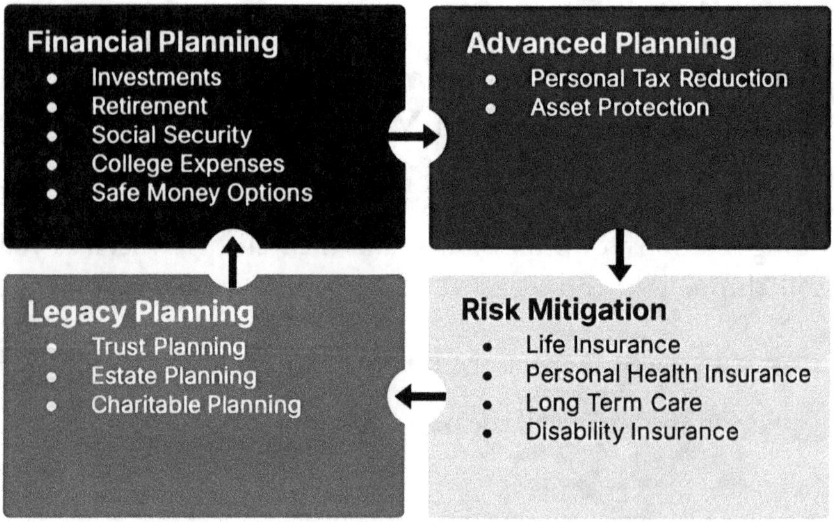

We next direct them to the **Business Planning area of the VFO Showroom.** Again, the image below shows only some of those solutions, and again, it's just a snapshot of the types of solutions available.

Virtual Family Office Showroom

Business Planning Focus

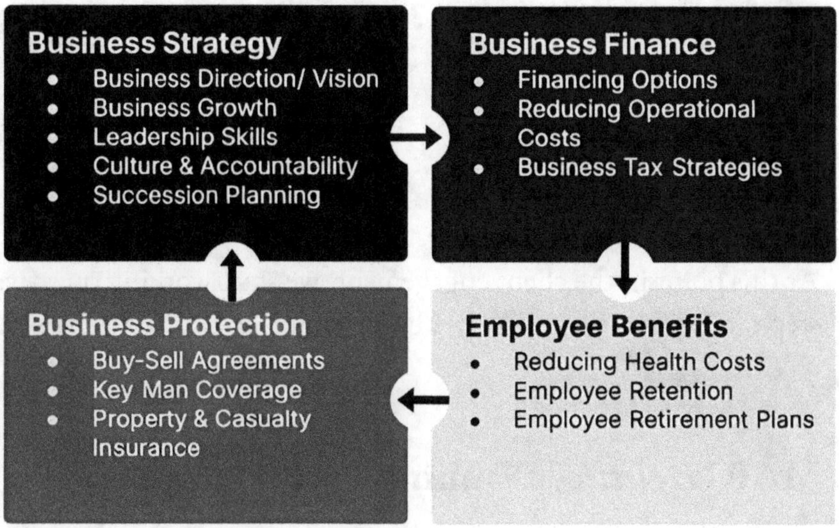

Overall, the **VFO Services Mission**, working with our Advisor Members is to proactively engage with clients to:

- Help them **Maximize Potential**
- Help become their **Most Relevant Proactive Advisors**

Together, we help clients **shape their future and add sustained value** via:

- Forward-Looking Advice
- Proactive Advice
- Value Added Solutions

Combined Proactive Planning and VFO

At this point in the client engagement, we start working on a five-step process that we call MAP. It is used for ***"Holistic Planning."***

MAP "*Holistic*" Planning Process

Big picture, there are two distinct phases to MAP which are:

- Proactive Planning Phase
- Solution Implementation Phase

We explain the key difference between those two phases to the client by suggesting they think of it like building a house. In that example, they would firstly employ an architect to design the house. That is the equivalent of the **Proactive Planning Phase** covering all the work that happens **BEFORE** a "shovel hits the ground."

In essence, this proactive phase of MAP is all about understanding what the client wants and educating them, as well as providing options on how to implement later.

The second, **Implementation Phase** only begins once the client has "reviewed the architect drawings" and "given the general contractor the greenlight to make it happen and start the build process."

Overall, we break MAP into five stages as follows:

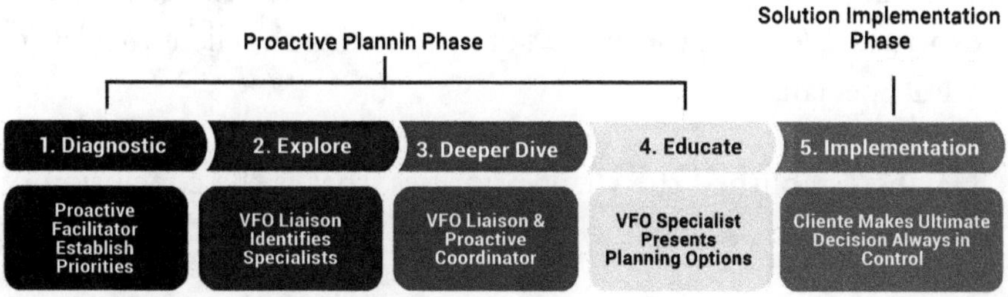

MAP Proactive Planning Process

Five-Step Process

MAP STEP 1 in the Proactive Planning Phase is the start point. We always begin with a **Diagnostic**, where we identify potential needs and establish the client's top priorities.

The Proactive Facilitator plays a key role in MAP STEP 1 and helps the client to complete the ***"Client Information Questionnaire" ("CIQ").***

The Proactive Planning Team uses the "CIQ" to establish and, ultimately, prioritize Personal and/or Business planning needs (of the client).

If the Advisor Team already has the skills to address their client needs directly, they will obviously do so (and it will feel like "business as usual").

However, where those prioritized needs fall outside the Advisor personal expertise, that is when we will need to introduce virtual expertise. We begin the process of introducing the client to relevant VFO Specialists.

Having established the client priorities, that is the conclusion of MAP STEP 1.

We cover in **Part 9** how to ***"Monetize"*** the engagement. However, for completeness, let us show you how the MAP process will continue through stages 2 through 5, assuming that we do "close," and the client wishes to move forward.

The job of Proactive Facilitator is complete, and assuming the client agrees to move forward, we would proceed to MAP STEP 2.

MAP STEP 2 is the hand-off from the Client Relationship Lead and Proactive Facilitator. This is where the **VFO Liaison and Proactive Coordinator**, together "pick up the baton" (and the "back office" starts to take ownership of the proactive process).

This second phase is where the VFO Liaison explores the Virtual Family Office Specialists to find the ***"right fit"*** **for the client's particular prioritized planning needs.** As you will appreciate, the VFO Liaison and Proactive Coordinator are very important in the Proactive Planning Team, albeit they are operating behind the scenes. You should think of them as being like ***"air traffic controllers."*** They are fundamental to the ultimate success of the process.

At VFO Services the **VFO Liaison:**

- Personally is involved in identifying all the VFO Specialists
  - VFO Services have more than seventy-five on our team
  - Contracting with them to ensure a seamless VFO Service

- The VFO Liaison knows all the Specialists personally
  - They meet with them regularly

- The VFO Liaison works with the Specialists to
  - Ensure the Specialists have the necessary information required to move forward on any particular case.

At the end of MAP STEP 2, the VFO Liaison moves to **MAP STEP 3.**

This step typically applies where the VFO Specialists need to "dive deeper." They likely require further details before they meet with the client (in MAP STEP 4).

It is at this point that the VFO Liaison "passes the baton" to the **Proactive Coordinator,** who will reach out to the client (or maybe, with client permission, to other professional advisors) to obtain that required additional information.

At the very least, the Proactive Coordinator will also liaise with all parties involved to set up the MAP STEP 4 Meeting where the client is introduced to the relevant VFO Specialist (as well as the Client Relationship Lead and often the Proactive Facilitator).

As you can see, the **VFO Liaison** and **Proactive Coordinator** are the ***"essential glue"*** to hold the process together and make things happen behind the scenes.

MAP STEP 4 is where the relevant parties meet to discuss the client's top priorities. This meeting typically involves:

- **Client**
- **Client Relationship Lead** *"holding the client's hand"* (The Advisor)
- **Proactive Facilitator** for continuity and to *"facilitate"* as required
- **VFO Specialist** to advise and *"educate"* on potential ideas and solutions

The VFO Specialist will **present different options to address the client's particular priorities.** They will advise with regard to what they consider to be the ***"best fit"* solution.** Their role is to **EDUCATE** the client.

In the meeting, the Specialist will cover both the **BENEFITS** (of a particular idea or solution) as well as outlining specific **IMPLEMENTATION COSTS** prior to the client being expected to make a final decision (as to whether to move to implementation in MAP STEP 5).

MAP STEP 4 is the final step in the **PROACTIVE PLANNING**

stage.

At the end of the meeting (or meetings, if more than one is required) the client will decide whether they would like to move forward to the **IMPLEMENTATION** Phase or need more time to review.

Overall, the **client engagement** message should be clear:

VFO Services always position the client as being ***"in control"*** of deciding whether to move to implementation in **MAP STEP 5** because there is a massive and fundamental difference between:

- **Proactive Advice and Discussion** (MAP 1-4)
    - *"Architect phase"*
- **Decision to Implement** (MAP 5)
    - *"General Contractor phase"*

That final step always requires specific terms of engagement to be completed prior to implementation of whichever solution is applicable.

This is the point where the "shovel hits the ground." We have moved from the intangible proactive planning phase (talking about maybe doing something) to the tangible implementation phase.

PART 8

Engage with Target Clients - Tax Planning

In Part 7, we described *"Holistic Planning,"* using MAP as our standard way to engage the client. That is our preferred way to begin the client engagement because we don't presume to anticipate client needs in advance, hence starting with the Diagnostic in MAP 1.

However, sometimes, and particularly with Tax Planning, the Advisor **already knows that their priority is tax planning.** The only real doubt is ***"what type of tax planning"***?

In that case, we use a different ***"TAX PLANNING"*** process described below to engage the client.

In addition to already knowing about the tax priority, there are two further, simple (but connected) reasons for tax planning being "different" than the standard MAP approach which are:

Tax planning is **COMPLEX**

- It feels like there are a *"million"* alternative tax strategies

Clients have different attitudes to tax planning **PERCEIVED RISK**

- All tax planning strategies are not equal (when it comes to risk)
    - Some tax strategies might be called *"vanilla"*
        - Typically, promise to save less tax - but "*don't push the envelope*"
    - Some tax strategies are more "*advanced*"
        - Typically, promise to save more tax - but "*do push the envelope*"

We will talk in more detail about the perceived risk later.

Tax Proactive Planning

Six-Phase Overview[3]

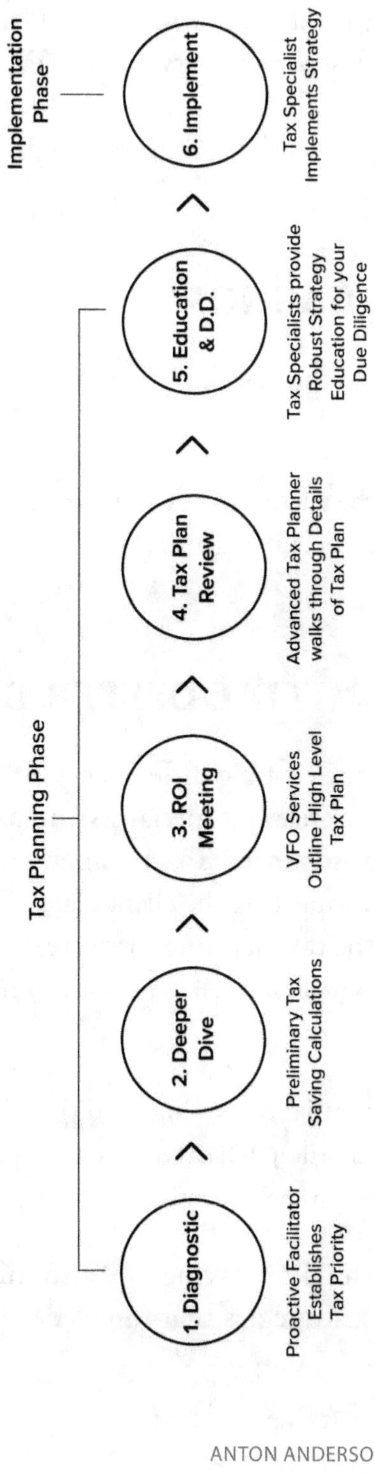
Tax Planning Phase
Implementation Phase
1. Diagnostic
Proactive Facilitator Establishes Tax Priority
2. Deeper Dive
Preliminary Tax Saving Calculations
3. ROI Meeting
VFO Services Outline High Level Tax Plan
4. Tax Plan Review
Advanced Tax Planner walks through Details of Tax Plan
5. Education & D.D.
Tax Specialists provide Robust Strategy Education for your Due Diligence
6. Implement
Tax Specialist Implements Strategy

As you can see from the illustration, The Tax Planning Process is six steps and (like MAP) separates between the **PLANNING** and **IMPLEMENTATION** Phases to allow the client to feel "in control" at all times. Let us run through the six steps at a high level.

TAX STEP 1 - DIAGNOSTIC

In this case, we use a specific Tax Fact Finder to replace the CIQ Diagnostic.

Either the Advisor or the client agrees to pay to VFO Services a small initial fee for the high-level tax planning work.

TAX STEP 2 - INITIAL DEEPER DIVE

This is where there is the first big difference with MAP 2. Instead of exploring the VFO for relevant specialists, in **Tax 2,** we advocate the use of a designated **Advanced Tax Planner** who carries out the initial *"deeper dive"* by inputting the client's latest Tax Returns (and other salient details) into the tax planning software (Elite and VFO Services both use TaxPlan IQ software in addition to our own proprietary spreadsheets and formulas).

This calculates the potential tax savings and the client potential return on investment (where their ROI is their net tax saving after the anticipated cost of tax planning and solution implementation).

Obviously those potential tax savings are also influenced by the types of potential tax strategies that might be employed by the client - which, in turn, links to the "risk mindset bucket" that the client prefers.

We need to explain this "tax risk mindset" in more detail.

Paul Latham told some interesting stories in the ***"Art of Proactivity"*** regarding clients having different mindsets to tax planning. Those stories illustrate the main point arising from any tax saving strategy, which is that:

Typically, the **more you *"push the tax envelope,"* the more complex the tax strategy usually becomes** (and the risk of objection from the IRS increases).[4]

To be clear, the above truism doesn't mean that somewhat "riskier" strategies are "bad tax strategies," or that the tax strategy will not ultimately be successful. However, advanced tax planning may well take longer to establish the position.

Consequently, the tax payer needs to be willing to accept the probability of greater scrutiny from the tax authorities (and the need for detailed paperwork where every "I" is dotted and every "T" is crossed).

For the client to become comfortable with a higher tax-risk mindset, strategies can require a certain "cojones," you might say. Obviously, it is important for the Client Relationship Lead and Proactive Facilitator to establish a risk mindset tolerance right from the start of the tax planning process. Not to do so is to invite problems later down the line (and probably waste an awful lot of tax planning effort).

Simplistically, at VFO Services (in the initial Tax Fact Finder), we ask clients to position themselves, and their mindset towards tax risk and complexity, into one of five broad "buckets" (see illustration below):

Tax Risk Mindset 1 to 5

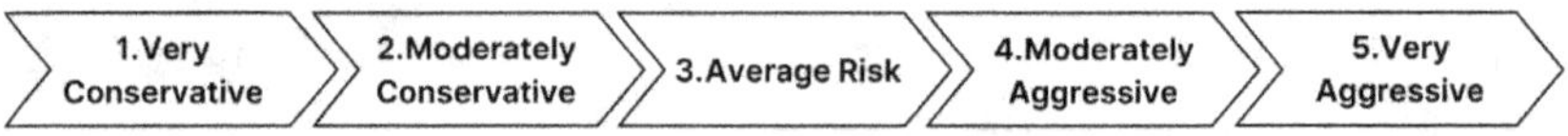

We should stress at the outset, that when VFO Services adopt a specific tax strategy, our due diligence process typically takes two months to complete, and for a strategy to be approved, it includes background checks, professional license verifications, and a complete documentation and research process. We require either tax opinion letters from tax attorneys or public letter rulings from the IRS. We have due diligence attorneys on retainer to assist and complete legal agreements and to protect everyone involved.

In short, VFO Services take this very seriously.

1. Very Conservative Strategies
   - Simple, safe, and long-standing
   - Only basic paperwork required to satisfy IRS
2. Moderately Conservative Strategies
   - Straightforward to set up and clear rules in place
   - Requires eligibility checks and simple math reviews
3. Average Risk Strategies
   - These have more *"moving parts."* Rules exist, and clients must follow details

- IRS will look at the underlying substance, structuring, and valuations.

4 Moderately Aggressive Strategies
- More complex strategies. Proper coordination required. Rules must be strictly applied.
- IRS will look at intent and pricing and require detailed documentation

5 Very Aggressive Strategies
- Very complex strategies and will require 8886 disclosures to IRS
- Elevated compliance burden and IRS scrutiny

The key to success with regard to the more aggressive risk strategies is to have experienced and knowledgeable high-level planners (like VFO Services Director of Advanced Tax Planning) and properly qualified and professional VFO Tax Specialists to implement the strategies and deal with IRS compliance, as required.

So, having explained the above nuances, let us return to **TAX STEP 2.**

As an example, if the client classifies themselves as being in "risk mindset category 2 or 3" above, it would be wholly inappropriate and misleading for the tax planner to consider potential tax savings and net ROI based on strategies that were more appropriate for (say) "risk mindset category 5."

It should be very clear that "one-size-does-not-fit-all" when it comes to Tax Planning.

TAX STEP 3 - *"ROI MEETING"* - HIGH LEVEL PLANNING

In every case, we start this part of the engagement by stressing to the client that the high level plan we are going to present is designed to maximize their return on their investment or *"ROI."*

The Tax Planner will consider from all angles, looking at retirement planning, "income shifting" deductions, entity-structuring, and "loopholes" and credits. Their focus is on balancing tax savings with sustainability.

VFO Services always charge for their services in line with AICPA guidelines (in fact typically at a 25% discount to their guidelines as a benefit to our Members and their Clients).

Design Plan to Maximize ROI

Consequently, you should now be really starting to fully appreciate why proactive tax planning is different than regular holistic planning (and an exception to regular priorities where we use MAP process) and why we use a different tax process (rather than MAP).

Continuing with **TAX STEP 3,** this is designed to be **HIGH LEVEL to allow the client to get comfortable at a gentle pace.**

The Tax Planner will:

- Outline potential tax savings
- Outline the *"risk profile"* of tax strategies proposed
- Ensure consistency with client attitude to risk
  - Adjusting risk profiling as necessary
- Outline the Tax Planning ROI Fee in principle

An important point to understand at the conclusion of Tax Step 3 is that the first 50% of the **Tax Planning Fee** becomes payable for **future planning** (detailed planning meetings with various Tax VFO Specialists). This is essentially a **retainer.**

The second 50% is paid upon moving to **TAX STEP 6** and final tax strategy **implementation**. If the client ultimately chooses not to move forward to the final implementation, then they won't pay that second 50%.

However, see the first guarantee that VFO Services provide upon payment of that first 50%. This is covered below in TAX STEP 4.

TAX STEP 4 - DETAILED PRESENTATION AND FIRST GUARANTEE

At this fourth step, the tax planner takes the high level plan, presented at TAX STEP 3, and breaks down the plan into the component details involved.

At VFO Services, we do offer a fee **guarantee** that if they are not comfortable after this detailed plan presentation, they can "stop the process" and obtain a refund of their initial 50% retainer.

TAX STEP 5 - CLIENT EDUCATION AND DUE DILIGENCE[5]

Assuming that they don't stop, the **initial 50% retainer becomes *"locked in"*** because, irrespective of final client decision on implementation, the client will have benefitted from the extensive work to educate the client and meet all the relevant VFO Specialists. That part of the engagement will have been completed.

This TAX STEP 5 is designed to allow the client **time to consider more deeply and, ultimately, firm up their preferences** from the range of tax planning ideas and possibilities. This is where the client does their ***"due diligence"*** prior to implementation - and they can take as long as they like to become comfortable.

Obviously, during these **Tax 5** meetings, we will continue to refine the client views on their tax risk mindset as they meet the relevant Tax Specialists. The key message is that the **client is *"in control"*** of their final implementation decisions (before moving to implementation in Tax Step 6).

TAX STEP 6 - IMPLEMENTATION OF TAX STRATEGIES

At this point the *"baton passes"* to whichever VFO Tax Specialists are driving any particular tax strategy towards implementation.

The VFO Services Tax Planner will continue to be involved through the implementation process, "holding the hand" of the client, to make sure that all proceeds smoothly.

As a **second guarantee** and comfort to the client, where VFO Services has committed to a projected ROI (net) savings that is not achieved, then part of the ROI tax planning fee will most likely be refunded (always calculated and presented in line with AICPA guidelines).

Tax Planning in Summary

Given the relative importance of tax planning to the typical client, it clearly deserved its own *"section"* in the client engagement process.

Furthermore, as can be seen, given the relative complexity of tax planning, it is an exception to the MAP process rule (albeit, there are clear and obvious similarities).

Nevertheless, it is the particular **impact of risk mindset tolerance upon tax planning** that represents the biggest difference with most other "regular planning priorities."

It is a foolish and probably inexperienced tax planner who doesn't place the client mindset towards tax risk tolerance "front and center" of their tax planning process.

PART 9

Monetizing the Engagement

The Price of Proactivity

How proactive do you want us to be?

Having diverted in Part 8 to also consider how to Engage in Tax Planning, let us now return to the more regular "*Holistic Planning.*"

In Part 7, we left this at the MAP 1 stage of the process, and we had just completed the CIQ Diagnostic and firmed up the client priorities (to work on in MAP 2 through 5).

One important aspect that we didn't mention in Part 7 is how to "***close the deal***" and how the **holistic and proactive services are priced** and ultimately ***"monetized."***

At Elite and VFO Services, we do our best to keep pricing comparatively simple, and we offer **three Proactive Service Level options**:

- ***"Proactive Lite"***
- ***"Proactive Core"***
- ***"Proactive Max"***

We normally outline the prices of these service levels in a quick follow up meeting, (after the "CIQ" Diagnostic and Prioritization process as detailed previously). Again, once we are in this Follow Up Meeting (arranged in Part 6), the Advisor makes the introductions as previously mentioned.

[ADVISOR NAME] starts the meeting by welcoming everyone to the call and asking the client how they are doing. Once the natural small chat concludes, the Advisor says, "Great, [PROACTIVE FACILITATOR NAME] why don't we go ahead and jump into things. Can you take it from here?"

PROACTIVE FACILITATOR TAKES OVER

Sure [ADVISOR NAME], I'd be happy to. Since our last meeting [CLIENT NAME], we reviewed your CIQ priorities and put together a few VFO Membership options we are excited to share with you. Let's jump into it.

Thereafter the Proactive Facilitator takes over. They will discuss with the client how we might **maintain the proactive conversation** with the client throughout the year (see Part 10) – as well as keeping the client up to date with ***"what's new and what's trending"*** in the proactive planning world.

However, the main reason we wait until the follow up meeting to discuss pricing is because we first need to ensure that we have **properly understood the client's top planning priorities, before we can settle on which service level and related pricing might be appropriate for them.**

Given that the initial meeting (in MAP 1) already takes about an hour (including the initial positioning presentation, completion of CIQ Diagnostic and establishing priorities), we feel that it is generally better to allow the client to take a break, and **review the pricing and look to *"monetize the deal"* with the client in a separate meeting** (ideally a pre-scheduled meeting two days after the initial meeting).

The main benefit of this pause is to allow the client to ***"sleep on their priorities"*** and feel comfortable with their decisions.

Now it is time to get more specific and more granular (and really define the proactive service).

Proactive Service Levels

How Proactive Do You Want Us to Be?

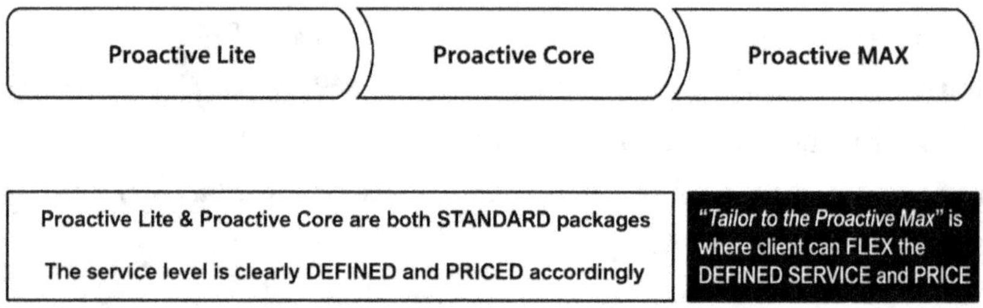

At VFO Services we include **three sub-elements** to the proactive advice service fee:

- **Membership of VFO Services**
- **Partners in Planning Meetings**
- **Priority Types** to be worked upon

Membership of VFO Services

Covers **standard services** that are always included:

- Access to VFO Showroom – and providing regular updates
    - ***"Twelve Months of Proactivity"***
- **Proactive Coordinator** Services – *"glue that hold process together"*
- **Contracting VFO Specialists** – to protect all parties involved

- **Administrative Services** – like invoicing, collecting monies

Partners In Planning Meetings

Covers **variable services** that fluctuate based on meeting frequency:

- Cover the costs of **Client Relationship Lead** and **Proactive Facilitator**
- They can be **fixed in advance** as standard
- *"Lite"* is one annual meeting / *"Core"* is four quarterly meetings
- The meetings can be **flexed through the year** in *"Max"* if required

Type of Priorities to be Worked Upon

Let's cover another type of **variable to the servic**e that fluctuate based on type of priorities to be addressed further to MAP 1

- VFO separate **Tax Planning Priorities** from all other *"regular priorities"*
    - With **Tax Planning** there is a small up-front fee to cover the time of the Director of Advanced Tax Planning in preparing initial high-level tax plan
        - This was covered in Part 7 Tax Planning
    - With **Regular Priorities** (everything except tax) – the cost is covered by the VFO Membership (see above)

Obviously, the **more priorities the client wants to address, the more proactive work there is to do** to identify the "right VFO Specialists." Through this pricing structure we encourage the client to maximize the benefit of their VFO Membership.

By using this three-sub-elements structure, VFO Services **define what is included in the Proactive Service** and **manage expectations** of the client by "putting it in a box" (as a defined proactive engagement).

Finally, depending on the type of service required by the client, at VFO Services we offer a **Membership Payment Plan** where:

- ***"Lite"* Membership** is paid in 1 initial sum
- ***"Core," "Max"* Memberships** are paid in 4 quarterly installments

We then capture everything in an **Engagement Agreement** - that ***"closes and monetizes the deal."***

At VFO Services, the final steps after the follow up meeting are driven by our **AI Proactive Coordinator,** where at the end of the follow up meeting, the Proactive Facilitator agrees the details with the client, the details of which are then provided to the AI Proactive Coordinator who, without human involvement, arranges:

- Draft **Engagement Agreement** - sent to the client
- Agreement Signed - Including **Fees and Payment Plan**
- **ACH Payment Details** provided by client

- Upon receipt of above - AI Coordinator will:
  - **Take the initial payment** - and email the client
  - **Generate an invoice** for the client
  - **Pay the revenue share due to the Advisor**
  - **Prompt the VFO Liaison to move to MAP 2**
  - As detailed in Part 7

Obviously, Advisors who wish to do this themselves (rather than use VFO Services), have access to the Elite Training Manual which includes a step-by-step guide to the above.

Having "closed and monetized the deal" let us move to Part 10 which covers, maintaining the relationship and generating further earnings via VFO.

PART 10

Maintaining the Relationship

Sustaining the Proactive Process

"Holistic and proactive for life – not just for Christmas Day"

Some of the biggest mistakes that inexperienced proactive and holistic Advisors make are:

1. They are too concerned about the short-term fees (from *Holistic Planning* or Tax Planning) and are **not mindful enough of the longer-term opportunities** and that there is a much *"bigger picture"* to consider when driving future VFO revenues.
2. They don't understand that the initial engagement (described in Part 7) is actually the easier part of the proactive process. **Sustaining the process** is the more challenging part.

With regard to the above, we have all heard the expression, "a dog is for life and not just for Christmas," and so it is with holistic and proactive planning, using the VFO.

VFO Services Facilitators and Advisors are trained to focus on a clear, two-fold **PURPOSE** that will maintain the relationship and drive future **VFO revenue generation.**

We want to **Maximize Client Financial Potential**

- Business and Personal Financial Potential

We want to become **Most Relevant and Proactive Advisor**

- The client's *"go-to-proactive team"*
    - Building a **deep - long-term - proactive relationship**

With regard to the latter bullet above, ***"most relevant"* builds further from becoming trusted.** Trust takes time to build. It is a long-term objective.

Trust requires sustained holistic and proactive effort on the part of the professional.

The easy part can be found in the initial steps (MAP 1 Diagnostic - Part 7).

In MAP 1, we are building from a ***"blank sheet of paper,"*** given that we don't know the client's priority needs. At that stage, we have a clear process to follow - using the **CIQ Diagnostic** and honing the **Proactive Priorities** and agreeing their **One Page Plan.**

To coin a phrase, being proactive in the initial stages is like ***"painting by numbers."*** If the Advisor and Proactive Facilitator follow the process, the proactive picture is pretty much guaranteed to become clear.

Furthermore, after that initial MAP 1, again, we have a clear engagement process as described in Part 7 and Part 8 (either MAP 2 through 5 for Regular Priorities or TAX 2 through 5 for Tax Priorities).

But what about the **NEXT** proactive planning meeting and the one after that and for **YEARS** after that?

At VFO Services, we call the regular meetings ***"Partners in Planning"*** or ***"PIP Meetings."*** Again, as in all things, we build on **PROCESS** and **STRUCTURE** to help the Advisor sustain the engagement.

A typical PIP Meeting would be structured something like this:

1. Review of Priority Progress since the last PIP Meeting.

At the initial ***"PIP 1"*** - the client will typically have chosen one or two priorities. If we are assuming that the client has chosen the ***"Proactive Core"*** service level, then their next planning meeting - ***"PIP 2"*** - will likely be in Q2 (about three months after *"PIP 1"*), so that is a good opportunity to assess progress with each priority identifying:

- VFO Liaison meetings with relevant VFO Specialists **(MAP 2)**
- Proactive Coordinator liaison to obtain key information **(MAP 3)**
- VFO Specialist meeting with client to educate as to opportunities **(MAP 4)**
- Any relevant progress with implementation as applicable **(MAP 5)**
- The above would be similarly the case with any tax priorities **(Tax 2 through 6)**

This is an opportunity for the Advisor to remind the client of substantive progress made (a key factor in starting to build trust and become Most Relevant Advisor).

2. Continuing the Proactive Discussion

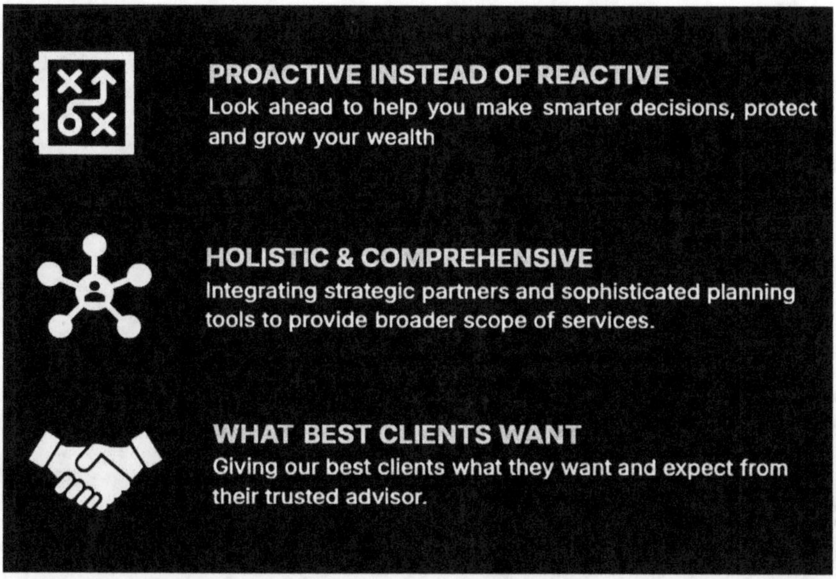

This is almost a new beginning to the conversation, a reminder to the client, that our goal is to be **PROACTIVE - HOLISTIC - COMPREHENSIVE** on their behalf.

What's new with you?

- Any changes we should be aware of?
- Any new problems?
- Any new opportunities?
- Anything on your mind?

We look to discover what has been happening in the life of the client in the last three months? Anything we need to be aware of?

Twelve Months of Proactivity

Topics Covered in Last Three Months

Example Month One

- Sell Side M&A/Exit Consulting
- Business Processes
- Business Financing
- Leveraged Deduction - Fee Simple

Example Month Two

- Payroll and HR
- Small Business Growth and Scaling
- Outsourced CFO Services

Example Month Three

- Leadership and Company Culture
- Cash Balance Plans
- Merchant Processing

Have any of the topics covered in the ***"Twelve Months of Proactivity"* Program,** since our last meeting, been of any interest to the client or "sparked their curiosity"?

We provide clients with a quick update on new VFO Specialists added to the VFO Showroom since we last met.

VFO Showroom Updates

VFO Showroom - *"What's Trending"*

- Energy Storage Tax Credits
- Business Scaling and Growth
- Business Processes and Systems
- Business Structuring: LLC, S-Corp vs. C-Corp
- Payroll and Health Insurance for Business Owners
- Estate Planning:
- Trust/Wills, Trust and Estate Documents, Irrevocable and Revocable Trusts

We show them areas of proactive planning that are proving to be popular - "trending" - with other high net worth clients "just like you."

All of the above topics are designed to help both the Advisor and client to **stimulate a fresh proactive discussion**. This pattern can be followed in all future meetings. We will quickly discover that we are building "proactive habits and routines," that without appropriate **MEETING STRUCTURE** would be more difficult to establish.

3. Any Changes to Priority Action Plan?

- Understand and Prioritize Needs
- Address Biggest Problems
- Achieve Most Important Goals

After "PIP 1," we established the client Priority One Page Plan. Any changes needed? Do we need to consider:

- **Existing Priorities Review** (further to part 1 of our Agenda)
    - Priorities we are continuing to work on (with no change to the plan)
    - Priorities to stop working on (to be removed from the plan)
    - Priorities we have completed (to be marked as completed on plan)
- **Parked Priorities Review** (further to *"PIP 1"* meeting)

- Do we want to upgrade any previously *"parked"* priorities?
- Do we want to drop any previously *"parked"* priorities (and remove them from our parked list)?
- Anything new that's come up today (to be *"parked until a later date")?*

- **Service Level Pricing Review** (further to previous pricing/ payment agreement)
  - Any changes required for new items?
  - Any refunds required?

4. Next Steps?

Typically, this will include updating other members of the Proactive Planning Team (VFO Liaison or Proactive Coordinator), confirming invoicing changes (since the retainer was agreed) or agreeing the date of the next *"PIP Meeting."*

If it wasn't apparent to you previously, the **key role of the Proactive Coordinator** in helping the Client Relationship Lead and Proactive Facilitator to prepare for these meetings is fundamental to sustaining the process smoothly and creating that "client engagement." As we have said before, they are the ***"glue that holds the holistic and proactive process together."***

PART 11

First Ninety Days and Creating Advisor Growth Plan

Getting off to a "*fast start*" and "*heading for your north star*"

Advisor 90 Day Plan

As outlined in the Executive Summary in Part 3, VFO FT is a "*done-with-you*" program designed to help you generate new revenue FAST.

That emphasis on ***"done-with you"*** starts from your initial **90 Day Plan**, working with Elite (before you start to work with clients and VFO Services), and your Member Success Manager.

The 90 Day Plan is a program designed to achieve fast results (typically requiring just two hours commitment per week) and to "hit the ground running."

The 90 Day Plan comprises twelve meetings (typically weekly but you can move faster if you want to), which are split into two phases:

- **90 Day Plan - Phase 1**
  - Training Meetings 1 through 4
    - Emphasis on understanding the training videos
    - Answering questions arising
    - Role plays
      - Inviting clients to planning meetings
      - Introduction scripts in planning meetings

Once you have successfully completed the above, you will be introduced to the VFO Services Proactive Facilitator, and from there will start meetings with clients (target is to start client meetings in less than thirty days from joining Elite).

- **90 Day Plan - Phase 2**
  - Activity and Accountability Meetings 5 through 12
    - Emphasis on **putting the training into action**
    - Monitoring progress
    - Creating good habits
      - It takes a minimum of six weeks to really build strong habits
      - 70% of adult learning is achieved by "*doing*"

Advisor Growth Plan

We never encourage Advisors to *"run before they can walk,"* but once it is clear to your Member Success Manager that you are successfully *"on your way"* with the basics of VFO Fast Track, the emphasis will shift towards helping you to build a longer-term Advisor Growth Plan (think of this as your *"North Star"* – linking to your vision).

Remember that we discussed the ***"three ingredients of business success"*** being **Vision x Plan x Desire.**

This is where theory turns to reality and the "rubber meets the road" – and you start to "put the pedal to the metal."

Your Member Success Manager will start to go further - building upon the initial weeks of training and discussion and getting to know you. We are going to create a Growth Plan designed to help you achieve your vision.

The Advisor Growth Plan is built around a tried and tested formula that we call ***"Only Four Ways to Grow"*** (business profits) – which are:

1. **Win New Clients** (or customers)
2. **Do More Transactions** (with existing clients)
3. **Increase Average Dollar Value** (of the average transaction)
4. **Get More Efficient** (increase profit margins or reduce costs)

The above represent fundamental business truths. You may recall the famous Lombardi phrase shown below about mastering the basics of football.

Master the Basics: Lombardi Philosophy

"Gentlemen, this is a football"

It is exactly the same with growing business profits, and there is a fundamental fact that to grow profits you must either:

- **Increase Revenues**
  - Achieved by some combination of **1)** and **2)** and **3)** above
- **Reduce Costs**
  - Achieved by **4)** above

Where individual Advisors will choose to concentrate will be reflected in their Growth Plan. Do you remember those ***"two***

businesses under one roof" that we introduced you to in Part 1? Here are some further business basics:

- **Business 1 - Advisor Core Factory**
  - Almost certainly you will focus on **1)** and **4)** above
    - You may choose to (say) win new core clients by:
      - *"Fishing with a single rod"*
        - That is traditional marketing via social media
      - *"Fishing with a big net"*
        - Read our sister book about **"Partnership Fast Track"**
    - You will want to get more efficient in the *"factory"*
      - Focus on eradicating the **"Seven Business Wastes"**
- **Business 2 – Proactive Planning *"Boutique"***
  - That is where we focus on **2)** and **3)** above
    - That is why we created VFO Fast Track to *"bolt-on"* to your business

However, again as we touched upon in Part 1, that separation above will bring structural issues and questions to answer like:

- Who will be ***"driving the factory"?***
  - Will it be Advisor (owner) – or somebody else on the team?
    - How does Advisor avoid *"Monday to Friday Syndrome"*
    - Where Advisor is delegating – what KPI's are needed
      - Advisor needs to feel comfortable - "let go of the wheel"

The big message is that the Advisor who wants to properly grow cannot possibly continue to "spin the business plates" alone, as sooner or later they will start to drop those plates! The way you have managed to grow the business to date – almost certainly will not get you to where you want to go (or where you want to grow more specifically).

How much value do you want to add in the *"boutique"*?

This sounds like a simple question (and it is simple in fact) – but it does need answering properly.

Whilst we have broadly explained the VFO Fast Track "planning boutique" as being a simple ***"second business,"*** that you can just "bolt-on" – it is actually sub-divided into two parts (described in Part 7 and Part 8).

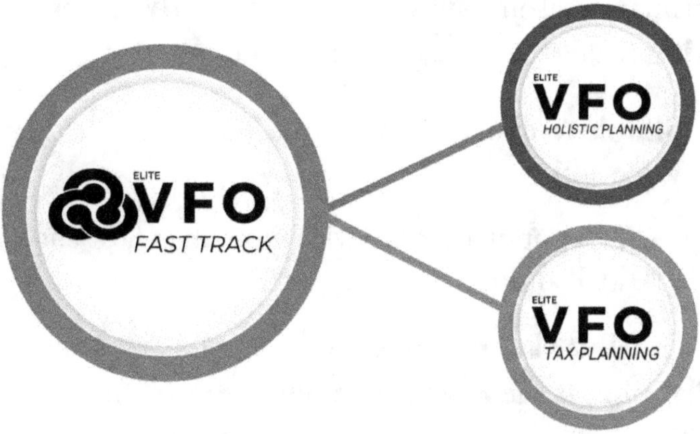

We went through this simply in Part 7 when we talked about **Holistic (MAP) Planning** (MAP 1 through 5 process), as compared to when we talked about the "exception to the rule" being **Tax Planning** (TAX 1 through 6 process) in Part 8.

In Part 8, engaging in Tax Planning, we were describing the exception in **terms of process** – and why that is necessary (mainly because of tax solution complexity).

However, that **separation also allows Advisors to choose**. When they do VFO Fast Track do they want to do:

- ***Holistic Planning* and Tax Planning**
  - Let Holistic lead and connect naturally to Tax Planning as clients choose their priorities
- **Tax Planning Only**
  - Described in Part 8 – Planning can start through a separate diagnostic, where the client already knows they need tax help

The primary reason why some Advisors **only choose the Tax Planning** (as their "second business"), is because:

- **Simple to explain** to Core Business Clients as a separate value-add
    - Most popular service with more than 80% choosing Tax Planning

However, the second reason (for the benefit purely of the Advisor) is that **Tax Planning is the most profitable** (for them and financially beneficial for the client). Tax Planning is more likely to result in "home runs" for the Advisor and Client, whereas Holistic Planning has a far greater chance of resulting in "singles – with maybe the occasional double."

Having said the above, the majority of Advisors recognize that by doing both **Holistic and Tax Planning they are offering their client *"best advice"* and fulfilling their fiduciary duty to the full**. They also recognize that successfully growing a business is also about "deepening the client trust and relationship" and not purely driven by money and profit.

Nevertheless, these are the type of deeper discussions that your Member Success Manager will be having as we build the Advisor Growth Plan.

Holding the Advisor Accountable to Implement Growth Plan

Remember the *"three ingredients of business success"*?

As Paul Latham used to say at Lathams Accounting – and we still say today at Elite:

- *"We can inject you with Vision"*

- *"We can inject you with Plan"*
- ***"We cannot inject you with Desire"***

The **Advisor has to bring their desire** – but we do help you by holding you accountable to deliver (and regularly update and revise) the Growth Plan you created. We achieve that by the use of accountability software (so we can see remotely as you "check off" your agreed tasks within the plan), as well as regular meetings with your Member Success Manager at Elite.

The message is clear. When Advisors have a strong desire to grow their business, then Elite has the Vision – Plans – Accountability to help you.

Conversely, if the Advisor cannot summon the desire to grow their own business, then we will not waste time trying to make them – ***"because you can take a horse to water, but..."***

PART 12

Next Steps – Your Journey Starts Now

Congratulations on reaching the end of our book. By this point, you have discovered the power of the Virtual Family Office, as well as how working with VFO Services can make achieving your vision quicker and easier.

We hope our message has:

- Increased your appetite to be a ***"proactive, forward looking"*** **Advisor**
  - For the benefit of your advisor clients
- Opened your eyes as to **how you can also grow your Advisor business**

To repeat what we said in the "Art of Collaboration," reaching the end of this book is not the end of your journey. Now, it's up to you to take the knowledge and insights you've gained, and put them into action. It's time to step out of your comfort zone, embrace change, and start to build the advisor practice of your dreams.

We know that change can be daunting, especially when you are venturing into uncharted territory. That's why we keep reminding you that you are not alone on this path. We're here to support you every step of the way, and so is the vibrant community of like-minded professionals as well as VFO Specialists, that we have built at Elite Resource Team.

If you are ready to "take a deeper dive," we invite you to join us at https://elitert.com/the-art-of-proactivity to access a wealth of exclusive resources, from templates, tools and technology, to coaching and training programs, and live events. Above all, explore our Virtual Family Office Specialists, who can help you to "look bigger," and with wider resources at a stroke.

As we have stressed throughout this book, the transformation journey is not always easy. There will be obstacles and setbacks along the way, and moments when you question whether it's all worth it. But we can tell you from experience, that the rewards from this path are beyond measure, both in terms of greater financial success, as well as the personal sense of fulfillment that comes from truly making a difference in your clients' lives.

Here's to your success and to the amazing things we know you will achieve.

Anton Anderson & Paul Latham

Frequently Asked Questions

Q1 - Explain the three types of Financial Advisor and how that impacts running a VFO?

As we explained in Part 2, very simplistically there are **three broad types of Financial Advisor**:

Those who have a vision to offer wider advice to their best clients (via the Virtual Family Office) – and are:

1. **Not overly constrained** by compliance factors
   • Can offer wider advice via VFO and ca**n accept revenue share f**rom VFO Specialists
2. **Somewhat constrained** by compliance factors.
   • Can offer wider advice via VFO but **cannot accept revenue share** from VFO Specialists
3. **Very constrained** by compliance factors:
   • **Cannot offer wider advice via VFO** regardless of revenue share arrangements

All three types of Financial Advisors typically want to provide access in some way to the VFO, but they have **different approaches and motivations.**

Type 3 - Very Constrained by Compliance Factors

This type is the easiest to understand. As outlined above, Type 3 Advisors cannot offer wider advice via the VFO, and nor can they accept any revenue shares.

Type 3 Advisors want to grow their core business, and that essentially means adding new clients who fit their particular "swim lane."

Forming a strong partnership with an Accountant is a great way for them to do this, as one of our colleagues Jon Kuttin (a Type 3 Advisor) likes to say, ***"it's like fishing with a big net."***

VFO Fast Track is perfect for Type 3 Advisors, because it means that they can help benefit the Accountant (via the gift of VFO Fast Track and access to VFO Services team), but they don't personally have to have any involvement with the VFO. In return, the Accountant will introduce the advisor to clients requiring traditional financial planning, while introducing clients needing other services to the VFO.

The **VFO Associate route is a total *"no-go"* for these types of Advisor,** as they are personally precluded from helping the Accountant to access the VFO.

Type 2 - Somewhat Constrained by Compliance Factors

This type is slightly more nuanced in terms of understanding their motivations. As outlined above, Type 2 Advisors can offer wider advice via the VFO, but cannot accept revenue shares.

Similarly to the Type 1 Advisors, they are **particularly attracted to the *"fishing with a big net"* concept** (to help win more core business clients).

Again, using VFO Fast Track (rather than the Associate route) is much cleaner for them because of their compliance restrictions, whilst the **VFO allows their clients to benefit from wider advice and best advice** (outside the Advisor's "swim lane").

This is exemplified by Dan Riso (Type 2 Advisor and Elite Member) who says:

> "My goals fit into the "two businesses under one roof" principle - ***I want to keep my core business boring and scalable*** (winning access to the right clients) - but I also like having a ***totally separate planning business which offers clean access to wider resources that support my more complex clients.*** Having access to the VFO Services team, means that I can hold the hands of my clients, and be able to ***orchestrate but not***
> ***have to execute the solutions."***

Type 1 - Not Overly Constrained by Compliance Factors

As outlined above, Type 1 Advisors can both offer wider advice via the VFO, and can accept revenue shares.

The VFO Fast Track allows these Advisors to **build *"two businesses under one roof,"*** but the ***"fishing with a big net"*** idea, **allows them to benefit from both core business introductions and introductions via the VFO.**

This is exemplified by Abraham Cecena (Type 1 Advisor and Elite Member) who says:

> "I love the 'two businesses under one roof' principle. I have chosen to concentrate my personal efforts on my core business, but the VFO Services team, working alongside a new VFO focused planning employee I have added to my team, means that I am aiming to 10x my business very quickly."

Q2 - What, exactly, does VFO Services Membership include for clients?

VFO Services Membership is an **annual membership,** which means that the client has:

- Access to all the **VFO Specialists** in the VFO Showroom.
- Access to **VFO Liaison** to help guide them to the *"right"* VFO Specialist.
- Unlimited work on client **Priorities** through the year (with the exception of Tax Planning where there is a small initial deposit required to cover initial high level tax review).
- Access to a **Proactive Facilitator for Partner in Planning Meetings** as required (number of meetings agreed at the point of engagement).
- Access to **Proactive Coordinator** who provides all administrative and client communication services.
- Access to ***"12 Months of Proactivity"*** updates, to help keep up to date with new proactive planning trends in the marketplace.

At the end of every twelve months we invite Members to renew their Membership. We also offer discounts for renewing Members.

Q3 - What guarantees and refunds does VFO Services offer?[6]

Depending upon the type of services provided, VFO Services offer various types of refunds and guarantees as follows:

- **Annual Membership**
  - Where VFO Client Members change their mind within thirty days of engagement we provide a full refund, no questions asked.
- **Core Service Planning Meetings**
  - Core Service includes four quarterly planning meetings through the year as standard.
  - Where the client wishes to discontinue any of those meetings part way through the year, we will refund the service amount relating to the meetings not held ($600 per unused meeting).
- **Tax Planning Fees - Guarantee 1**
  - This is described in detail in Part 8 (see Tax Steps 3 and 4).
    - At **Tax Step 3** we provide the client with a high level plan, outlining anticipated ROI in line with the client's agreed tax risk mindset.
    - At **Tax Step 3** we agree an overall Tax Planning Fee and we initially invoice 50% of that total as a retainer
    - At **Tax Step 4** we then move into presentational detail to go through the *"nuts and bolts"* of that high

level plan. If for any reason at that point the client wishes to stop, we provide a full refund of that initial 50% paid. This is **Tax Guarantee 1.**

  - Assuming the client wishes to continue with the process through **Tax Step 5**, meeting the various VFO Specialists, discussions with their other professional advisors and completing their due diligence prior to implementation, that means they have entered the **Education and Due Diligence Phase.** Having done so, they no longer qualify for a refund or Guarantee 1 as described above, because VFO Services are incurring considerable costs during that Education Phase.

- **Tax Planning Fees - Guarantee 2**

  - Again, described in detail in Part 8 (see Tax Steps 5 and 6).

    - At the conclusion of **Tax Step 5, where the client confirms that they wish to move from Education and Due Diligence to Implementation (Tax Step 6).** They pay the second 50% invoice due (further to agreement in principle in Tax Step 3 above).

      - If the client wants to stop after Tax Step 4 there is nothing further to pay

    - At **Tax Step 6** we move into the **Tax Strategy Implementation Phase.**

    - This is led by the applicable VFO Tax Specialists, however, the VFO Services Team will continue to *"hold the hand"* of the client through the process.

- However, once implementation is complete, where the actual ROI achieved is not in line with anticipated ROI (at Tax Step 3), we will provide a refund in line with ROI actually achieved (where we are fully compliant with AICPA guidelines). This is **Tax Guarantee 2.**

At VFO, we describe the above as our ***"double tax guarantee".***

Overall, and notwithstanding the above specifics, at VFO Services, we take client satisfaction very seriously, and where a client in exceptional circumstances has a legitimate grievance, then we will always default to ***"doing the right thing,"*** and if that requires a refund then so be it. Equally, clients should expect to pay properly for advisory services provided in good faith.

Q4 - Who leads Specialist meetings with the client?

In Part 7 we describe the proactive process that we call MAP 1 through 5 where:

- **MAP 1** - initial diagnostic
- **MAP 2** - identify *"right"* VFO Specialist
- **MAP 3** - ensure VFO Specialist has required information
- **MAP 4** - meet VFO Specialist - Education Phase
- **MAP 5** - engage VFO Specialist - Implementation Phase

In Part 8 we describe how that process is slightly different with Tax Planning.

However, in both cases it is the Education Phase (**MAP 4 or TAX 5**) where the client first meets the VFO Specialist.

In those meetings the VFO Specialist will technically ***"lead the discussions,"*** as after all, this will be their particular area of expertise. However, there will always be a VFO Services team member present to help ***"facilitate the discussions."*** This will typically be the Proactive Facilitator for regular priorities or Director of Advanced Tax Planning for tax related priorities.

Either way, at VFO Services, we strongly believe in ***"holding the hand"*** of the client through the proactive process, to ensure that the client can make the "right decision" for them. Ultimately we facilitate the discussions to allow the **client to feel *"in control"*** - and **not feel like they are being *"sold to or pushed into implementing by any VFO Specialist."***

Q5 - How long before clients see value from strategies?

This will obviously vary by the type of strategy.

Many **regular strategies are very simple**, and the client might see value in only a couple of weeks, or months.

By contrast, **some strategies, like tax planning, are more complex.** As a result, their value may be felt in a few more months.

Irrespective of type, our goal is to balance two factors:

- **Drive value to the client as quickly as possible**
- **Allow the client sufficient time to make up their mind prior to implementation** and not feel rushed or *"sold to."* We want the client to feel *"in control"* at all times.

As always, at VFO Services we seek to achieve the "right balance" between speed, client experience and generating results.

Q6 - Can you explain the timelines/cadence and the difference between Lite or Core Service Levels?

The timeline or cadence in **Lite or Core** is simple (we cover in Part 7 of the book).

Both Lite or Core start from the same place at the **Initial Partner in Planning** or ***"PIP Meeting"*** where we:

- Introduce the **VFO Concept**
- **Complete the Diagnostic**
  - First pass to establish a *"long-list"* of potential priorities
- **Finalize One Page Plan**
  - Second pass to narrow to a *"short-list"* of immediate priorities
    - Any other priorities can be *"parked"* to action later
- **Agree Service Level**
  - Complete Engagement Agreement and Payment Plan

Having completed the above we are effectively at the start of Q1 of a 12 Month Membership. The VFO Liaison will then start working on the immediate priorities. The activity in the remainder of Q1 will be determined by the number of priorities agreed above. Also see FAQs # 7-8-9-10-11 for other related considerations around this area.

If the client chooses **Core Service** - then they will have 3 more quarterly Partners in Planning meetings in Q2 - Q3 - Q4.

We colloquially call those meetings "PIP 2, PIP 3, PIP 4." In Part 10, we outline the format of each of those meetings - but typically the Agenda is:

- **Review Progress**
  - Confirm actions with previous priorities (see above)
- **Continue the Proactive Discussion**
  - Anything new impacting your life
  - Discuss what's trending in the proactive world
  - New VFO Specialists - with new areas of expertise
- **Update the One Page Plan**
  - Agree items to prioritize moving forward

The above cadence would be repeated across Q2-Q3-Q4.

Where one of the above quarters coincides with "tax planning season," it is likely that particular emphasis will be placed there at that time.

Overall, the key difference between Lite and Core is the frequency of proactive meetings (annual versus quarterly), which allows the client to build a deeper relationship with the Advisor and Proactive Facilitator.

At VFO Services we are pleased to note that on average 77% of clients choose Core, because they prefer more regular meetings with the team, even though that service costs slightly more than Lite.

Q7 - Explain in detail the process for establishing priorities?

This is further to the CIQ Diagnostic process that we briefly outlined in Part 7 (and also touched on in FAQs #4 and #6 above).

Establishing client priorities is a two-part process, where we start at a **high-level** (creating an initial long-list of possible priorities) and then "drill down" to clearly **establish the client's top priorities** (which ideally then becomes a short-list, see below).

Part 1 - CIQ Diagnostic – "First create a long-list of possible priorities"

Effectively the **CIQ is a series of planning prompts at a high level.**

The Proactive Facilitator walks through a number of questions in the CIQ (approximately thirty-five questions in total), to obtain a **better understanding** (initially at a high level) of the client's **planning needs and concerns.**

The questions are organized within the usual five main areas of the Virtual Family Office:

- Business Advisory
- Tax Planning
- Risk Mitigation
- Wealth Management
- Legal Services

Typically, we will gauge the client's level of interest in any particular area (not interested, somewhat interested, very interested and so on).

This first, high-level, part of the process typically takes about fifteen minutes to complete. It is basically only a ***"first pass"*** in terms of understanding client needs.

Part 2 - Establishing Top Planning Priorities – "Then focus on the short-list"

This is where we take the above ***"first pass"*** list and really ***"hone it,"*** between immediate priorities and other items (which were of interest) are for **later down the line** (essentially, they are planning areas that are "parked" for a later date).

Priority One Page Plan - Proactive Planning

HAVING COMPLETED:

- ✓ Client Information Questionnaire to identify areas of interest
- ✓ Prioritization Process to determine immediate / later areas of focus

IMMEDIATE PRIORITIES

- Income Tax Planning
- Estate Tax Planning

We will begin to address these priorities with immediate affect.

PARKED PRIORITIES

- Business Growth
- Trusts & Wills

We will reconsider these priorities at our next Partners in Planning Meeting.

This is where the skill of the Proactive Facilitator becomes apparent.

A weak Proactive Facilitator (the type who are more interested in "selling" rather than establishing needs) may allow the client to pick "too many" priorities. As with "Goldilocks and the Three Bears" there is a "just right" number. We cover this in more detail later in the book.

This second part of the process, again, typically takes about fifteen minutes to complete. It allows us to finalize the client ***"Priority One Page Plan."*** At Elite and VFO Services, it looks like this:

The One Page Plan clearly establishes with the client that we have followed a **2-part Holistic Process, comprising:**

- (1) **CIQ Diagnostic**
    - Establish initial areas of interest to the client
- (2) **Prioritization Process**
    - Determine top priority areas of focus
        - Agree which areas to *"park"* for later discussion
- It is **transparent** to the client what we are proactively focusing on
- It is **re-assuring** to the client that we are focusing on their needs (not *"selling watches"* – see FAQ #8 – but we have not forgotten other areas of interest (and parked priorities for a later date)).
- We are **proactive for the client's benefit** (we are not proactively selling for Advisor benefit - again see FAQ #8).

Q8 - What do you mean by being proactive for the client's benefit rather than the Advisor's benefit?

We are talking about being **proactive for the client's benefit** (and not proactive for our benefit as Advisors).

At Elite and VFO Services, we pride ourselves on helping our trained members to aim to become **Most Relevant Advisor** to their clients. That position is only reached through **establishing trust and providing long term, and sustained value** to clients.

As we say at Elite, if you want to build a trusting relationship, you must ***"never sell a watch"*** to the client.

Nobody wants to be *"sold a watch"* (anything you don't really want or need). That sale may be described as being "proactive," but it is better described as proactivity for the benefit of the sales-person – the person "selling the watch."

Instead, you obviously want somebody to be proactive for the client's benefit. That client needs somebody to "step outside their personal silo," and help the client to **take a holistic view**, and become their **Most Relevant Advisor**. Somebody who always does the "right thing" for **THEM** (not for you the Advisor).

Furthermore, part of doing the "right thing" means helping them by **not trying to tackle too many priorities simultaneously** (see FAQ #12).

Q9. How do you price *"advice"* separately from *"solutions"*?

To answer this question, we will take you through some of the Elite learning fundamentals over FAQ #9 and #10 and #11. We are showing this across 3 questions, to help break the thinking down step-by-step.

After working in this area for over a decade at Elite (and learned over thirty years ago at Lathams by Paul Latham) Anton and Paul understand several things:

Elite Learning 1: Advice is Valuable and SEPARATE

- **ADVICE should always be SEPARATED from SOLUTIONS**

Paul Latham learned at Lathams Accountants in the 1990's, that it is better from the client perspective to **treat proactive advice as a separate product in its own right,** and not to try and "bundle" advice, together with other specific solutions and services.

In this way, the **client can see very clearly what they are paying for** (at any stage of the process). They then have **two clear decisions to make**. Do they want to:

1. Pay for **PROACTIVE ADVICE** – to be **EDUCATED** on possibilities?
2. Pay for a **SOLUTION** to be **IMPLEMENTED**?

It's clearly poor advice (and definitely not in the best interest of the client) to try and create an engagement covering both (1) and (2) simultaneously, because, **by definition, the client cannot know the answer to (2) before they have been advised on (1).** It is that simple.

Furthermore, If the answer to (1) is that they do want that "proactive advice" service, then the supplementary question becomes, ***"exactly how proactive would you like me to be?"***

The proactive advice service needs to be defined (see Learning 2 below in FAQ #10). Advice is an "intangible" service, and should not be pre-ordained to be "one size fits all."

At VFO Services, we offer choices around the question "how proactive do you want me to be"?. We offer:

- ***"Proactive Lite"*** – for **minimum** proactivity
  - Includes one proactive planning meeting per year
- ***"Proactive Core"*** – for **standard** proactivity
  - Includes four proactive planning meetings per year
- ***"Proactive Max"*** – for ***"tailoring to the maximum"***
  - Tailored number of meetings to suit the client needs

And as we explained in Part 9 we then price the service levels based on three variables:

- **VFO Services Annual Membership**
  - See FAQ #1 for details

- **Number of Proactive Planning Meetings**
- **Type of Priorities**
    - Regular priorities included in Membership
    - Tax Planning requires a small initial deposit

Q10. How do you define the level of proactive service?

Paul Latham learned at Lathams, to make any intangible service (like holistic and proactive advice) as ***"clear as a Coca Cola shaped bottle."***

Paul Latham also talks about defining the service, by mentally thinking about "putting it into a box."

That means really **defining what the proactive advice service includes** – and more importantly, being transparent as to what it **does NOT include**.

That is exactly why VFO Services use the MAP 1 through 5 process to make the distinction clear between **ADVICE PHASE** and **SOLUTION PHASE** (which is a similar concept to the TAX 1-6 process).

MAP Proactive Planning Process - Five Step Process

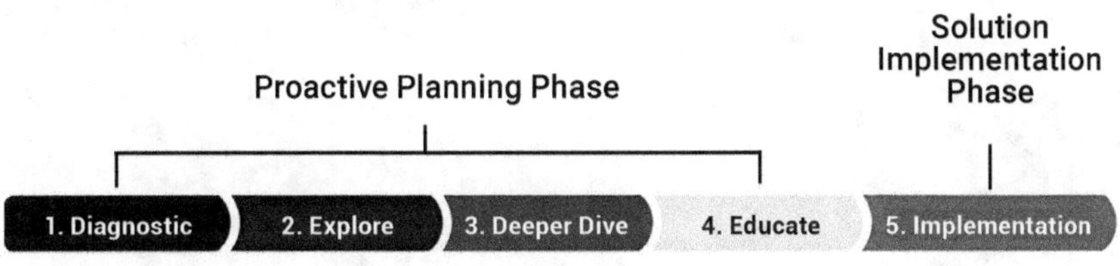

You will remember, as shown in the illustration above, there are 2 phases of MAP:

- **Advice Phase** – MAP 1 through 4
- **Solution Phase** – MAP 5

In terms of defining the proactive service - and "putting it into a box" - the proactive advice service **INCLUDES MAP 1 through 4** but **EXCLUDES MAP 5.**

The result is that the client has a **separate decision** at the conclusion of MAP 4, whether to **SEPARATELY ENGAGE** the VFO Specialist to **IMPLEMENT SOLUTION** (we discuss this further in Elite Learning 3 below in FAQ #11).

Consequently, the first step is to know that the MAP 1 through 4 steps we previously detailed are "inside the proactive service box" and MAP 5 implementation is "outside the box of service," as it will vary by whatever service is implemented.

Q11. Why don't we include solutions in the proactive pricing?

Elite Learning 3: Avoid including *"Uncertain Solutions"*

This is really just an extension of Elite Learning 2 (in FAQ #10), which is all about defining what the proactive service **does include.**

Learning 3 is about emphasizing what the proactive service **does not include**.

We strongly believe at Elite and VFO Services that it is a huge mistake to try to ***"crowbar"* any inherently uncertain solution into a fixed fee proactive advice service price.** That approach is flawed and doomed to failure (more often than not).

Obviously, by this "crowbar" method, less scrupulous professionals are hoping to "sell" a particular solution that they want to offer (by "bundling" it into the overall proactive service).

However, the truth is you **SHOULD NEVER** include a (MAP 5) solution, "bundled" with the MAP 1 through 4 service because until the client has decided to move forward, that solution is **NOT CERTAIN** to always happen.

To paraphrase what we said in FAQ #9, It's clearly poor advice (and definitely not in the best interest of the client) to try and create an engagement covering both advice and solutions simultaneously, because, **by definition, the client cannot know if they want that solution, before they have been advised on what the solution involves.** It is that simple.

Q12. What are the optimum number of client priorities (at any one time)?

The quick answer is that it is obviously hard to totally generalize, but at VFO Services we do strongly recommend that the Proactive Facilitator tries, as far as possible, to limit the number of priorities they are working on with a client (at any point in time).

Generally, the client should NOT try to tackle too many priorities simultaneously.

The reality is that, whilst trying to tackle more than (say) two priorities (max three) at any time may seem "good for the professional" (because they are "selling watches" and will likely result in additional VFO Revenues), it is actually counter-productive when it comes to building long-term client trust.

Quite honestly, allowing any client to push for more than two to three top priorities simultaneously is a demonstration of a very poor, inexperienced and weak facilitator. They are merely "selling watches" and **NOT providing best advice to their clients** (see FAQ #8).

Part of the ***"Art of Facilitation"*** is to help the client **minimize priorities** (ideally two any point in time – and then "park" others and return to them at an agreed later date).

Those "parked" priority items allow professionals to come back to the client at a later proactive meeting (say in Q2-Q3-Q4 etc.) as a part of ***"sustaining the proactive conversation"*** **over months and years.**

Also, from the client perspective, trying to tackle too many priorities simultaneously will **likely become unmanageable** (and the client will be less likely to enjoy, or continue, the proactive process).

As in the story of "Goldilocks and the Three Bears" (eating their porridge):

You don't want porridge that is "too cold" or "too hot," you want that porridge "just right." We believe two priorities at any time (maybe three at a push) is most likely going to be "just right."

Q13 - Can Members adjust VFO Services pricing to clients?

Yes, VFO Services proactive pricing is **flexible within boundaries.**

Member preferences on pricing should be determined as part of the **role play training discussions** (ideally not on a case by case basis).

Different Types Of Priorities

Regular Priorities

- Standard pricing assumes a 50:50 split with the Member.

Tax Planning

- Standard pricing assumes a one-third share paid to Member

Member wishes to charge less than standard price

The Member can choose to do so, but the VFO Services share will remain as their Standard Share (50% if Regular and two-thirds if tax planning). This is because VFO Services are only paid for this service via the revenue share - and the work to be done across MAP 1 through 4 or TAX 1-6 cannot be effectively completed, at the appropriate level of quality, if the VFO Services share is less than their standard share.

Member wishes to charge more than standard price

The Member can choose to do so on *Holistic Planning* only and the increase is shared as standard (it is too complicated, with too many ramifications to increase on Tax Planning).

Best Practice on Proactive Pricing

As you can see above the pricing is flexible, but the VFO Services position is that **we do not really recommend flexing.** Again, we follow the *"Goldilocks and Three Bears"* approach - not too low - not too high - but instead aim to get it *"just right."*

Remember - VFO Services is providing a "free extra" service for Members - and VFO Services only generates a revenue share upon successful conversion. However, notwithstanding the above, we **strongly believe that the real aim of the VFO Fast Track process is a combination of two elements:**

1. **Initial Conversion - Start the proactive conversation**
   "Help the client to understand benefit of proactive advice"
2. **Sustaining the proactive conversation**
   A continuing, deeper relationship needs to be formed *"Because a dog is for life and not just Christmas Day"*

Q14 - Can a Member choose to offer only Tax Planning Services and not *Holistic Planning*?

Yes, we discussed this in Part 11 where we introduced the image below.

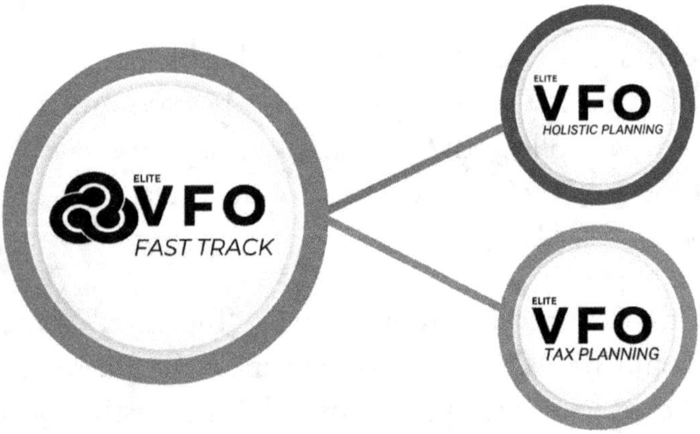

That **separation also allows Advisors to choose** whether they want to do:

- ***Holistic Planning* and Tax Planning**
    - Let Holistic lead and connect naturally to Tax Planning as clients choose their priorities
- **Tax Planning Only**
    - Described in Part 8 – Planning can start through a separate diagnostic, where the client already knows they need tax help

The primary reason why some Advisors **only choose the Tax Planning** is because:

- **Simple to explain** to Core Business Clients as a separate value-add
    - Most popular service with more than 80% choosing Tax Planning

However, the second reason (for the benefit purely of the Advisor) is that **Tax Planning is the most profitable** (for them and financially beneficial for the client). Tax Planning is more likely to result in "home runs" for the Advisor and Client, whereas Holistic Planning has a far greater chance of resulting in "singles – with maybe the occasional double."

Having said the above, the majority of Advisors recognize that by doing both **Holistic and Tax Planning they are offering their client *"best advice,"* and fulfilling their fiduciary duty to the full**. They also recognize that successfully growing a business is also about "deepening the client trust and relationship" and not purely driven by money and profit.

Nevertheless, ultimately this is a decision for the Member.

Q15 - How do VFO Services qualify clients for Tax Planning Services?

As outlined in Part 8, and Part 11, and further to FAQ #14, there are two ways that clients can access Tax Planning Services. They either come through from:

- ***Holistic Planning*** - where they identified tax planning as a priority during a Partners in Planning Meeting

Alternatively, they came directly through

- **Tax Planning** - where the **client already knew tax was a priority**

Irrespective of route, at VFO Services we have a key criteria for qualification which is the client **Adjusted Gross Income** or ***"AGI."***

In addition to the above, we also take account of other factors, for example a client may have a low AGI, but we may also be aware that they have a recent or pending ***"capital tax event"*** (like the sale of a business interest).

Essentially what we are looking for is good reasons to do tax planning, which is ultimately driven by two factors (described in Part 8) which are the client's:

- **Potential Return on Investment (ROI)**
    - Tax saving as a percent of the cost of strategy implementation

- **Mindset towards Tax Risk**
    - Determines the *"right tax strategy"* for client peace of mind

At VFO Services we will only start tax planning in any detail where we believe that we can generate a **minimum of 200% ROI** (double your investment in the tax saving), where the applicable strategies are in line with client **Tax Risk Mindset.**

This approach is really "common sense" and is a more sophisticated extension of "not selling the client a watch" as outlined in FAQ #8.

Q16 - What happens if a client's advisors / CPA object to a particular tax strategy?

At VFO Services we always seek to work in collaboration with the client's other advisors (most commonly their CPA).

This is part of the reason that we have the TAX 1 through 6 process as described in Part 8. To remind you it is shown in the next page.

TAX STEP 3 is where we are typically talking to the client at a **HIGH LEVEL**.

We outline their potential ROI - hence why this meeting is called by VFO Services the ***"ROI Meeting."*** We are determining if the client is interested - and also comfortable with the investments required to achieve that ROI (planning fees and strategy implementation, and also cashflow timings required).

TAX STEP 4 is where we take the client into a **DETAILED PRESENTATION.** If the client is not comfortable after this presentation they can stop the process and obtain a refund (see Guarantee 1 as detailed in FAQ #3).

TAX STEP 5 is where we are seeking to **EDUCATE** and allow the client to do their **DUE DILIGENCE.** That due diligence absolutely includes providing the client an opportunity to involve their other advisors as applicable (including CPA). If the CPA is very uncomfortable, and the client decides to stop the process, they can do so (See the tax guarantees we outline in FAQ #3).

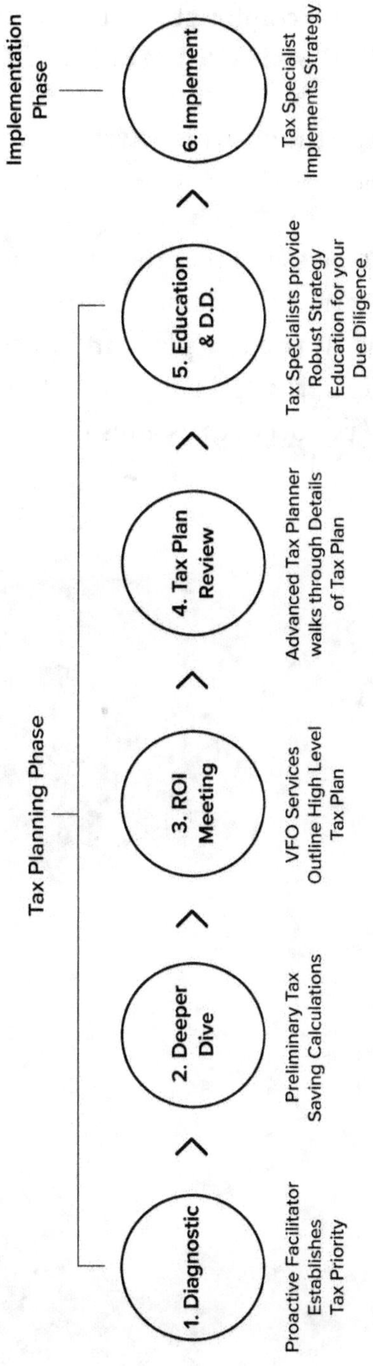
Tax Planning Phase
Implementation Phase
1. Diagnostic
Proactive Facilitator Establishes Tax Priority
2. Deeper Dive
Preliminary Tax Saving Calculations
3. ROI Meeting
VFO Services Outline High Level Tax Plan
4. Tax Plan Review
Advanced Tax Planner walks through Details of Tax Plan
5. Education & D.D.
Tax Specialists provide Robust Strategy Education for your Due Diligence
6. Implement
Tax Specialist Implements Strategy

Only when the client is comfortable with a particular strategy do we move to **TAX STEP 6 - IMPLEMENTATION.**

The message is clear, the **client is always in control** (and that includes being influenced by the views of their advisors and CPA).

However, in reality, we find that the vast majority of the time, we are not only educating the client, we are **also educating those other advisors as to the tax planning possibilities**. In fact on numerous occasions, the CPA will wish to develop a deeper relationship with VFO Services as a result, for the benefit of their other clients.

Q17 - How are VFO Tax Specialists vetted (why were they chosen and what is the due diligence process)?

The process for introducing new VFO Specialists is similar across all five areas of the VFO (irrespective of whether tax focused). However, it is fair to say that we place extra emphasis on tax strategies.

With regard to how a new **VFO Specialist is chosen initially,** they usually come from recommendations relating to a particular industry specialist. Those may come from other Members or from other VFO Specialists, or any other educational source that our VFO Liaison investigates.

With regard to the **due diligence process,** the illustration below is an extract from one of the slides that we go through with every tax planning client at VFO Services.

Tax Planning Details

VFO SPECIALIST ONBOARDING GUIDE

1. Initial Vetting & Credential Verification
2. Compliance & Risk Management
    - Require third-party documentation evidencing strategy legitimacy:
        - Private Letter Ruling (PLR) from the IRS, or
        - Formal Tax Opinion Letter (TOL), or
        - Independent legal due-diligence report (e.g., Mick Law).
3. Technology & Data-Security Alignment
4. Process & SOP Alignment
5. Capacity & Scalability
6. Economics & Engagement Terms
7. Client Experience & Educational Resources
8. Formal Approval & Integration

The Proactive Facilitator reminds the client in the meeting that our team will have previously touched on the due diligence we do prior to approving VFO Specialists.

Now, as we start to go deeper on the tax planning strategies, we always want to give the client more insight on the tax planning specifics.

Our due diligence process typically takes two months for any particular tax strategy to be approved, and may include background checks, professional license verifications, and a complete documentation and research process.

There are typically multiple zoom meetings to ensure that the Specialist aligns with the Elite and VFO Services mission and core values. When it comes to Tax Planning, the Advanced Tax Planner becomes heavily involved, probing and asking questions around economic substance, documentation and history of a particular strategy.

At VFO Services, when a tax strategy is being reviewed, we require either tax **opinion letters from tax attorneys** or **public letter rulings from the IRS.**

In addition, we have **due diligence attorneys on retainer to assist, and complete legal agreements to protect everyone involved.**

There are a lot of industry terms on the slide illustrated above, but in short, at VFO Services we take the due diligence process behind VFO Specialists, and particular tax strategies very seriously.

Q18 - Explain how the contractual situation works between all the parties involved (how does that impact revenue sharing and what the client pays for a particular service)?

This answer needs to be provided from a wide perspective to truly arrive at the appropriate context.

When the VFO Liaison brings on a new VFO Specialist, they actually do several things. They consider the Specialist from several perspectives (not only revenue sharing).

- **Due Diligence** perspective
  - See FAQ #17 above
  - **Member Needs** perspective
  - Does the new Specialist fill a *"gap"* in the VFO Showroom?
- **VFO Specialist** perspective
  - Will the VFO Specialist benefit from being added to the VFO Showroom? Is it likely to be worthwhile for them?
- **Contractual** perspective
  - They need to agree to fit in with the tri-party contractual structure at ERT and VFO Services (see below)
- **Revenue Sharing** perspective
  - It needs to be a *"win-win-win"* for the three parties to the arrangement

In terms of the questions asked, let us particularly concentrate on the last two areas above.

Contractual Perspective

At Elite and VFO Services, we have a **tri-party contractual structure** that are ***"mutually symbiotic."***

An example of a mutual symbiotic relationship is where say, "a clownfish gets protection from sea anemones while cleaning them," or "where bees pollinate flowers while gathering nectar."

We build a relationship where three parties win (four win including client):

- The **Member** - and their **Client**
- The **VFO Specialist**
- **Elite Resource Team / VFO Services**

The contracts all link together to achieve this - and it works as follows:

1. **ERT (including VFO Services) and Member contract**
    - Elite agree to provide access to three things
        - Coaching and Communities
        - Tools and Technology
        - Access to VFO Showroom
            - Includes option to do this via VFO Fast Track

However, we stress in the above contract, that when we provide access to the VFO Showroom we are **making an INTRODUCTION** to the VFO Specialist and Member.

2. ERT (including VFO Services) and VFO Specialist contract

Essentially we repeat the above clarity in terms of what ERT are providing the VFO Specialist - where again Elite are **making an INTRODUCTION** to the VFO Specialist and Member.

It is very transparent and both parties understand totally - as well as the Revenue Sharing arrangements as detailed below.

3. Member's Client and VFO Specialist contract (engagement agreement)

Once the Client (of the Member) moves from MAP 4 through 5 or from TAX 4 through 5 then they are moving from **ADVICE** to **IMPLEMENTATION.** The client is in control and they engage the VFO Specialist.

The level of the **implementation fee is agreed between the Client and the VFO Specialist**. Albeit the VFO Services team have a "good handle" on what might be regarded as "normal rate for the job" and can advise the client accordingly.

Similarly the VFO Specialist knows that we know their "normal rate." They also know that if we are not happy with them, we are unlikely to send them any future work.

It is the definition of a mutually symbiotic relationship where everybody wins from the above tri-party contractual relationships.

Revenue Sharing Perspective

Part of the VFO Liaison's job in bringing on a new VFO Specialist is to agree the revenue share that Elite will receive (further to the Specialist contract with the client in contract three above).

Each revenue share detail will vary in its amount, because of different industry norms. The VFO Liaison will always try to seek a balance between what is "fair and reasonable" to provide a sustainable relationship. It's a combination of **what is fair** to:

- **VFO Specialist** - this is effectively a cost of doing business for them (like a marketing cost)
- **Elite / VFO Services** - we are doing all the *"leg work"* to make these arrangements, and monitor everything that happens.
- **Member** - in terms of what they could achieve by themself

Generally, and irrespective of the dollar amount paid by VFO Specialist to Elite (the gross revenue share), we will then in the first instance pay 50% of that gross to the Member as a revenue share (compliance permitting), leaving Elite with a net 50% share in the first instance.

However, if the Elite share (from a particular Member) over the course of a calendar year builds beyond targets and tiers, Elite will pay an ever increasing **Rebate** and **Membership Credit Notes** to that Member to reward success.

Q19 - What does the Proactive Facilitator actually do?

The main role of the Proactive Facilitator is to facilitate meetings, typically in four entirely different circumstances:

- **Initial Partner in Planning Meetings (PIP 1)**
    - Leads the client through the process of identifying and prioritizing their planning needs
        - VFO Services facilitators are extensively trained, and heavily practiced in presenting the process to clients.
- **Subsequent Partner in Planning Meetings (PIP 2-3-4)**
    - Sustains proactive process and deepens client relationship
        - Reviews Progress since last meeting
        - Prompts further proactive discussion
        - Updates One Page Plan
- **Introduces VFO Specialists to client (MAP 4)**
    - Holds the client hand in meetings and ensures that VFO Specialists do their job to:
        - Educate the client
        - Provide options and alternatives
        - Explain costs and benefits clearly
- **Presents High Level Tax Plans to client (TAX 3)**
    - Positions the Advanced Tax Planner to succeed (in TAX 4)
        - Presents the outline plan and potential ROI
        - Explains the retainer fee structure
        - Explains the guarantee structure

Q20 - What does the VFO Liaison actually do?

One of the main jobs of the VFO Liaison is to **onboard new VFO Specialists** (as detailed in FAQ #17). In addition to that the VFO Liaison is also involved with:

- **Monitoring the quality of the VFO Specialists**
  - They are actively looking for signs of both good / poor work
  - They will particularly investigate any complaints and act accordingly
- **Point Members towards appropriate VFO Specialists**
  - Think of this like a *"concierge"* in a hotel
  - Make introductions as necessary
- **Monitoring the status of VFO *"Deals"* working through pipeline**
  - They will liaise with both Members and Specialists on progress
- **Ensuring that VFO Specialist Revenue is accounted for properly**
  - Reconciling from invoices payable to bank receipts
  - Allocation of monies received to a particular Member or Members
- **Ensuring that Member Revenue Shares are accounted for properly**
  - Ensuring that appropriate payments are made
  - Ensuring that Monthly Statements are sent to Members

- Ensuring that annual Member Rebates and Credit Notes are calculated - and eventually paid - properly.

In addition to the above, the VFO Liaison will work with the **Elite Executive Team** (Anton and Paul), in terms of monthly communication with the **Advisory Board.** This is a **non-executive team**, comprising the 5 most successful Members from the previous calendar year (in terms of monies generated from the VFO).

The Advisory Board offers suggestions to the Executive and VFO Liaison in terms of any potential improvements regarding how the VFO functions.

Q21 - What does a Proactive Coordinator actually do? How do you do this at VFO Services?

At VFO Services, we describe the Proactive Coordinator as the *"glue that holds the proactive process together."*

As a generality, a Proactive Coordinator is responsible for the following:

- Ensuring that **meetings happen,** coordinating times and zoom appointments between clients, team members and VFO Specialists.
- Ensuring that **communication happens** after meetings, so that everyone is clear on *"next steps."*
- Ensuring that other members of the team and VFO Specialists have the **appropriate client information at their fingertips**, and where necessary reaching out to clients to get further information.
- Ensuring that **billing and administration** is kept up to date, to include:
    - **Client Engagement Agreements** are:
        - Drafted - Sent - Signed by all parties - Filed
    - **Invoices are generated**
        - Covering the annual membership and future meetings and agreed priorities
    - **Payments are received**
        - With respect to the above invoices, including the quarterly payments where Core Services is chosen

- **Member Revenue Shares are paid**
  - These should be paid in line with agreed sharing percent and immediately after client payments are received

Obviously the above is a complex exercise, especially when you consider that at VFO Services we have hundreds of Members using VFO Fast Track, each of who may have dozens of clients using the proactive service.

At VFO Services, most of these tasks are done **automatically by an AI Proactive Coordinator** (who is programmed to do all the above based upon simple inputs by other members of the team). Please reach out if you want further information about the benefits of an AI Proactive Coordinator.

Q22 - How is the client billing / Member revenue share handled?

We explained this in overview in FAQ #21, but drilling into slightly more detail, the **answer is by process.**

That process starts from having agreed revenue share splits (see FAQ #13).

At VFO Services the standard shares are:

- **Holistic Fees** - split 50:50 with Member
- **Tax Planning** - split one third with Member
    - This can vary depending upon the degree of Member involvement in actual planning and implementation (the above assumes the Member has no involvement)
- **VFO Revenues** - split 50:50 with Member
    - In addition, the most successful Members receive annual rebates and Membership Credit Notes as rewards for generating revenues in excess of agreed targets and tiers

Having agreed the above, it is then a simple task to track client activity (again using AI Proactive Coordinator as referenced in FAQ #21). As a payment is received (from the three broad types highlighted above), the AI Proactive Coordinator allocated the monies in line with the percent shares, and payment is made promptly.

In addition at the beginning of each calendar month, every Member receives a **Summary Member Statement,** that itemizes each "deal" completed in the previous month, with the amount of money received and the appropriate Member Share. This information is split between **Prior Month Activity - Year to Date**

Activity - Annual Rebates and Credit Notes accrued in the year to date.

At VFO Services we believe in **100% transparency** when it comes to Member Revenue Sharing.

Q23. What skills make a good Proactive Facilitator?

At VFO Services we are a strong advocate of using DISC profiling. We covered this in some detail in the *"Art of Collaboration."*

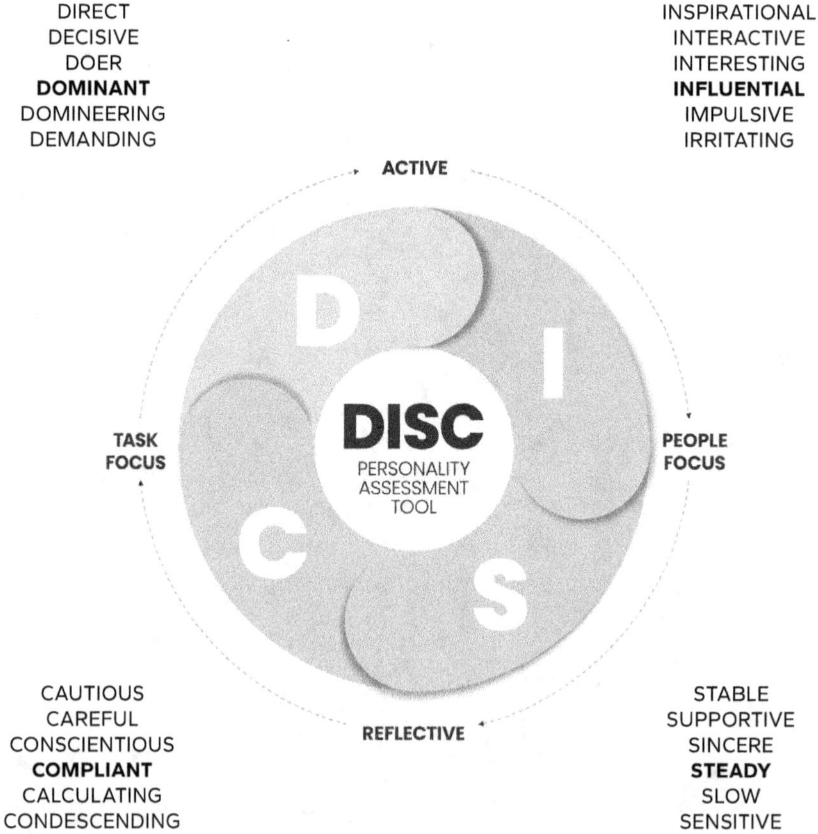

As we said in that previous book, the Proactive Facilitator must have:

- **High I**
    - Influencing and Facilitation skills
- **Low S**
    - Open to change - the opposite of *"steady"* in the image

Although the above are key and obvious, in point of fact it is likely to be the **relative position of the D** and their degree of "directness" and "doing" that will determine success.

For example, a very high I but a very low D will likely equate to a "social worker" (with all due respect to social workers!). What we want is a **High I** but also at least a ***"medium D"*** to not only influence and facilitate, but to **make things happen and make some decisions.**

At VFO Services, we believe that the above traits are significantly more important than a deep knowledge of all the available VFO Specialists. That is the job of the VFO Liaison, and not the job of the Proactive Facilitator. That is why at VFO Services we separate MAP 1 from MAP 2.

- **MAP 1** - the Proactive Facilitator identifies needs and **INFLUENCES agreed priorities** and steers to a **DECISION** on One Page Plan
- **MAP 2** - the VFO Liaison identifies the *"right"* VFO Specialist required

Q24. What detail do you include in a Proactive Engagement Agreement?

VFO SERVICES

Membership Service Agreement

CLIENT: **Test Client**	EMAIL: **test@test.com**
ADDRESS:	
PHONE NUMBER:	

Dear Test Client,

In order to document the understanding between us as to the scope of the work that we will perform, we are proposing this Agreement with you. To avoid any misunderstandings, this Agreement defines the services we will perform for you as well as your responsibilities under this Agreement.

Proactive Core Service Level

We will perform the following services:

Partners in Planning (MAP 1)

- Annual Diagnostic

- Thought Leadership — "12 Months of Proactivity"
- 3 Additional Planning Meetings throughout the year (quarterly in Q2, Q3, and Q4)

Planning Priorities

- 3 Initial Planning Priorities to be worked on ASAP
- Additional Planning Priorities beyond the initial priorities established in MAP 1

Exploring the Virtual Family Office (MAP 2–3)

- VFO Liaison discusses priorities with Specialists
- Proactive Coordinator coordinates where "deeper dive" required (setting meetings and obtaining more information)

Proactive Education Meetings (MAP 4)

- Client meetings with VFO Specialists
- Provide solution implementation quotation
- Ensure Client "in control"

Fees & Payment Terms

Annual Fee for Proactive Core: $5,400

$1,350 Initial Payment, followed by 3 quarterly payments of $1,350

Payment 1 — Due Upon Receipt

Payment 2 — Due June 25, 2026

Payment 3 — Due September 23, 2026

Payment 4 — Due December 22, 2026

*The previous payment dates can be adjusted based on the date the initial payment is received.

Unanticipated Services

If an unanticipated need arises we agree to perform the additional work at a mutually agreed upon price. This service will be billed separately and will be payable upon presentation.

Satisfaction Guarantee

We provide a 100% Money Back Guarantee on Proactive Core and Proactive Max service levels. If you are unhappy with your choice and would like your investment back, please let us know within 30 days of signing this agreement and we will refund you 100% of the amount paid to date.[7]

Indemnification

You agree to and shall indemnify and hold harmless all liabilities which arise out of, in connection with, or related to: (i) any breach of this Agreement by you; or (ii) any action or inaction of any other professionals.

To assure that our arrangement remains responsive to your needs, as well as fair to both parties, we will meet through the year and, if necessary, revise or adjust the scope of the services to be provided and the prices to be charged in light of mutual experience.

Furthermore, it is understood that either party may terminate this Agreement at any time, for any reason, within 10 days of written notice to the other party. It is understood that any unpaid services that are outstanding at the date of termination are to be paid in full within 10 days from the date of termination.

What We Expect From You

Please initial each section to indicate that you agree with these statements.

__________________________I am willing to be an active participant in the Proactive Planning process. I understand that each part of the process requires information or participation from me. I promise to stay engaged because I understand the outcome of my plan hinges on my cooperation and involvement.

__________________________ I agree to be responsive to emails and phone calls within a reasonable period of time. I understand that many tax and financial planning issues are time sensitive.

__________________________ I agree to provide requested data and documents in a timely fashion. I know that if I leave you waiting, I am only hurting the planning process.

__________________________I understand that if there are any expert, investment, or coaching fees, they would be agreed upon in advance. We work with a systematic process one step at a time, so there will never be surprises.

Acknowledgment & Acceptance

If you agree that this proposal adequately sets forth your understanding of our mutual responsibilities, please authorize this Agreement.

You will find the timeliness and quality of our services to be unmatched. We express our appreciation for the opportunity to serve you.

Please feel free to contact us if you have questions regarding any portion of this Agreement.

Sincerely,

________________________ ________________________

Signature Date

Anton Anderson

VFO Services

12636 High Bluff Dr, Suite 400

San Diego, CA 92130

Accepted and Agreed:

____

Client Signature

________________________ ________________________

Print Name Date

Q25. What detail do you include in the Tax Engagement Agreement?

VFO SERVICES

Tax Planning Engagement Agreement

CLIENT: **Test Client**	EMAIL: **test@test.com**
ADDRESS:	
PHONE NUMBER:	

Engagement Agreement for Tax Planning Services

Dear Test Client,

We are pleased to confirm our engagement to provide you with comprehensive tax planning services under our Proactive Tax Planning framework (described below). This letter outlines the scope of services, responsibilities, timing, and fees for our engagement.

Proactive Tax Planning Framework

Our services are phased across 6 steps as follows:

Steps 1 to 3. Initial Tax Plan Design at a High Level

- Development of a customized tax plan aligned with your goals and your **Tax Risk Mindset (Risk 4 - Moderately Aggressive Mindset).**
- Analysis of opportunities in deductions, entity structuring, credits, retirement planning, and income shifting.

Step 4. Detailed Tax Plan

- Meeting with Director of Advanced Tax Planning to present the proposals in detail and ensure that you are comfortable in principle with the proposed strategies (see Guarantee 1 detailed below).

Step 5. Education & Due Diligence

- Education sessions to ensure you understand each strategy.
- Collaboration with specialists (tax, legal, retirement, and others as appropriate).
- Provides opportunity for you to complete your due diligence prior to final implementation.

Step 6. Implementation Support

- Coordination of tax strategy implementation with applicable tax specialists.
- Ongoing support during Year 1 to ensure proper execution.

Client Responsibilities

To enable us to provide effective planning, you agree to:

- Provide timely and accurate financial, tax, and business information.
- Engage and compensate any third-party specialists required to implement specific strategies (e.g., tax credits, legal structuring, retirement plans, etc.).
- Make decisions regarding implementation in a timely manner.

Fees & Payment Terms

Total Tax Planning Fee: $21,000

The terms of this payment are:

Retainer — $10,500 payable upon execution of this agreement (Prior to Step 4)

Implementation Fee — $10,500 payable once the Education and Due Diligence in Step 5 is complete and tax strategies agreed upon (Prior to Step 6)

Additional costs may include:

- Investments in energy tax credits or other tax credits.
- Third-party professional fees (e.g., attorneys, actuaries).
- Contributions to retirement plans (which remain your assets).

VFO Services "Double Guarantee"

Guarantee 1. If you are not satisfied with the detailed tax plan as presented in Step 4 (above) and decide that you do not want to move forward to Step 5, we will refund 100% of the initial retainer as quoted in this Tax Engagement Agreement.

Guarantee 2. If you move forward with implementation in Step 6 (above), but the tax savings are lower than projected, we guarantee to "*make it right.*"[8]

Term & Termination

This engagement begins upon signing and remains in effect until the completion of Year 1 tax planning implementation. Either party may terminate with written notice; refunds will apply per the guarantees outlined above.

Indemnification

You agree to and shall indemnify and hold harmless all liabilities which arise out of, in connection with, or related to: (i) any breach of this Agreement by you; or (ii) any action or inaction of any other professionals.

Acknowledgment & Acceptance

Please confirm your agreement by signing below. We are excited to help you capture significant tax savings and build a strategy that keeps more of your wealth where it belongs — with you.

Sincerely,

________________________ ________________________

Signature Date

Anton Anderson
VFO Services
12636 High Bluff Dr, Suite 400
San Diego, CA 92130

Accepted and Agreed:

____

Client Signature

________________________ ________________________

Print Name Date

Endnotes

1 Net worth figures reflect publicly available estimates at the time of writing (early 2026) and are subject to change.

2 The five strategies listed on pages 42, 43, and 44 are examples only. Tax laws are subject to change. Individual suitability varies based on personal financial circumstances. Consult a qualified tax or legal professional before implementing any tax strategy.

3 The tax planning process described in this section is for educational purposes only. Tax laws and IRS regulations are subject to change. This content does not constitute tax or legal advice. Consult a qualified tax professional before implementing any strategy.

4 Advanced tax strategies may carry additional complexity and regulatory scrutiny. Always consult a qualified tax advisor before proceeding.

5 The tax planning process described in this section is for educational purposes only. Tax laws and IRS regulations are subject to change. This content does not constitute tax or legal advice. Consult a qualified tax professional before implementing any strategy.

6 ROI projections are estimates based on individual client circumstances and are not guaranteed. Actual tax savings will vary depending on personal financial situation, applicable tax law, and implementation outcomes. This guarantee applies solely to VFO Services fees paid and does not constitute a guarantee of specific tax savings or investment returns. Consult a qualified tax professional before engaging in any tax planning strategy.

7 This guarantee applies solely to VFO Services membership fees paid and does not constitute a guarantee of any specific financial, tax, or investment outcome. Individual results will vary.

8 *"Make it right"* refers to a fee adjustment to take into account the difference between projected and actual tax savings, subject to the terms of this agreement and applicable AICPA guidelines. It does not constitute a guarantee of specific tax savings or investment returns. Actual tax outcomes depend on individual financial circumstances, applicable tax law at the time of implementation, and factors outside VFO Services' control. This guarantee is limited to fees paid under this engagement and does not cover third-party costs, specialist fees, or implementation expenses incurred by the client.

www.ingramcontent.com/pod-product-compliance
Lightning Source LLC
LaVergne TN
LVHW022218200926
848481LV00006B/2019
* 9 7 9 8 9 5 0 5 8 3 1 0 0 *